Cape Breton
Pictorial
Cookbook

Photography by Warren Gordon, M.P.A.
Edited by Yvonne LeVert, Cordon Bleu Chef

Published by: Steel Town Publishing
Gordon Photographic Ltd.
367 Charlotte Street, Sydney, Nova Scotia Canada B1P 1C8

Design: Jacqueline Ranahan

Canadian Cataloguing in Publication Data   ISBN 0-9690395-3-0

CONTENTS

INTRODUCTION

Cape Breton Island stretches out before the eye like a patchwork quilt. On the island, the beautiful art of interwoven threads and pieces of fabric stitched in intricate designs and patterns has won acclaim for the quilters of the area. These quilt designs have been handed down from generation to generation. Many of the early quilts are now family heirlooms.

The cuisine of Cape Breton can be compared to the intricate design and stitching of a quilt. It is a celebration of cultural identities of the various ethnic groups who have settled here. They came for whatever reason, bringing with them treasured recipes, techniques and traditions of many backgrounds. Among them were Highland Scots, Acadians, Irish, English, Italians, Polish, Ukrainians, Lebanese, Europeans, Africans, West Indians… They lived alongside the Mi'kmaqs who were permanent residents of the land. In time, some melding of these diverse cultures and identities began to take place, but for the most part these settlers retained their religious and ethnic traditions.

Few events in communities and parishes are held without a focus on food. Enjoyed are the flavours, fragrances and textures of special food for special occasions and celebrations. The "down home" approach to cooking is characterized by a simplicity and goodness that relies on the freshness of local ingredients. To that end the opening of the lobster season is comparable to a national event! Rare are the people who would not respond with delight to a bowl of seafood chowder, a "mess" of salt cod and pork scraps, a succulent roast leg of lamb or a bowl of fresh strawberries and cream.

The foods in this pictorial cook book are as wide-ranging as they are original and delicious. Many are old favourites such as oatcakes, boiled dinners, poached salmon, and tea biscuits served in homes and food establishments on the island. For a sensory cultural experience, try Kibbi, Maragan, Rosotto, Fricot, Hodge Podge, Jerk Chicken, Irish Stew, Knishes, Stovies, or Paska. This melting pot of ethnic variety provides a rich patchwork and identification of what the cuisine of Cape Breton is all about.

Inspired by the wealth and variety of natural delights and other ethnic riches found locally, the Cape Breton Chefs featured offer a selection of foods that will tempt even the most sophisticated palate, and will provide the readers with new and innovative ideas and techniques. These foods are representative of the cuisine served in eating establishments throughout the island.

Through his lens, Warren Gordon has taken us on a cultural voyage where magnificent and breathtaking scenery is rivaled only by a splendid overlapping of bountiful banquets rich in variety and tradition. Together we offer a delicious and distinctive celebration of Cape Breton cuisine.

Enjoy!

Yvonne LeVert

Yvonne C. LeVert

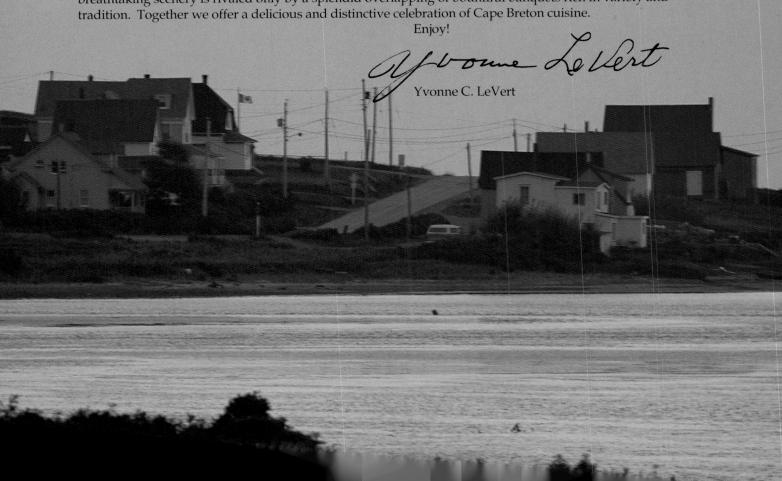

MI'KMAQ
Collected by MRS. MARGARET JOHNSON,
ESKASONI

RABBIT STEW

1 Rabbit, skinned, cut in pieces
3 Large Carrots, thickly sliced
1 Small Turnip, cut in large pieces
6 Med. Potatoes, cut in pieces
1 Large Onion, sliced
1 Bay Leaf
1 Clove Garlic
1 Tsp. Salt (5 ml.)
1 Tsp. Pepper (5 ml.)
6 Cups Cold Water (1.2 L.)

Sponge cut up pieces of rabbit with damp paper towel.
Arrange pieces of rabbit in a large saucepan and cover with
cold water. Add onion, bay leaf, garlic, salt and pepper.
Bring to a boil and cook until rabbit is almost tender. Add
turnip and carrots. Cook for 10 minutes. Add potatoes and
cook until all is tender. Thicken the broth mixing 3 Tbsp.
(45 ml.) flour with 1/2 cup (125 ml.) of cold water. Shake
well together and add to rabbit stew. Mix well and cook until
broth is transparent and thickened.

EEL STEW

2 Eels, skinned
1 Small Turnip, sliced
1 Onion, chopped
6 Potatoes, cut in pieces
1 Clove Garlic
1 Tsp. Salt (5 ml.)
1/2 Tsp. Pepper (2 ml.)
8 Cups Cold Water (2 L.)

Cut skinned eels in approximately 2 inch pieces. Place pieces
in saucepan. Cover with cold water and bring to a boil.
Reduce heat to simmer and cook for 30 minutes to tenderize
and cleanse. Drain. In a large saucepan put sliced turnip,
garlic salt and pepper. Cover with cold water, bring to a boil
and cook until turnip is partially cooked. Add the potatoes
and eel and continue cooking until tender.   *Serves 6.*

DUMPLINGS

1 Cup Flour (250 ml.)
2 Tsp. Baking Powder (10 ml.)
1 Tsp. Salt (5 ml.)
1 Egg
1/2 Cup Milk (125 ml.)
2 Tbsp. Oil (30 ml.)

Combine milk, egg and oil. Add flour, baking powder and
salt and mix to a stiff batter. Drop from spoon over stew.
Cover and cook dumplings for 7 - 10 minutes until firm.

MI'KMAQ HASH

2 Inch Square Salt Pork (5 cm.)
1 Onion, sliced
1 Clove Garlic
6 Medium Potatoes
1 Tsp. Salt (5 ml.)
1/2 Tsp. Pepper (2 ml.)
3 Cups Water (750 ml.)

Cut salt pork in slices and fry in a skillet to render the fat.
Add onion, garlic, salt, pepper and potatoes. Cover with
water and cook until potatoes are tender.   *Serves 4 - 6.*

GINGER CAKE

3/4 Cup Oil (175 ml.)
3 Eggs
1 Cup Granulated Sugar (250 ml.)
2 Cups Molasses (500 ml.)
4 Cups Flour (1 L.)
2 Tsp. Salt (10 ml.)
1 Tbsp. Ginger (15 ml.)
1 Tbsp. Cinnamon (15 ml.)
2 Tsp. Nutmeg (10 ml.)
1 Tbsp. Baking Soda (15 ml.)
3 Cups Raisins (750 ml.)
3 Cups Hot Black Tea (750 ml.)

Beat together oil, eggs, sugar and molasses in a large bowl.
Measure flour, salt, ginger, cinnamon, nutmeg and raisins
together. Dissolve soda in hot black tea. Fold dry ingredients
into egg mixture alternately with the black tea. Beat well for
1 minute until batter is smooth, yet thick. Grease a large roast
pan and spread batter evenly over pan. Cover and bake in a
350°F (180°C) oven for 1 hour or until tester comes out clean.
Yields 12 large pieces.

FOUR CENT CAKE

2 Cups Flour (500 ml.)
3 Tsp. Baking Powder (15 ml.)
1 Tsp. Salt (5 ml.)
1 Cup Cold Water (250 ml.)

Mix flour, baking powder, salt and water together.
Form mixture into a ball and knead on a floured board for
2 - 3 minutes. Divide dough into two pieces and flatten into a
circle with hand. Heat 2 Tbsp. (30 ml.) of oil in a large skillet.
Fry cakes 5 minutes on each side. When cooked cut in
wedges and serve as a bread.   *Makes 8 - 12 wedges.*

TOP: Mi'Kmaq basket and Quillework   ABOVE: Indian Islands, Eskasoni   OVERLEAF: Fortress Louisbourg

7

FORTRESS LOUISBOURG

DRIED PEA POTAGE

2 Cups Dried Peas (500 ml.)
1/2 Cup Dried Kidney or Navy Beans (125 ml.)
1 - 1 1/2 lb. Ham Butt (500 - 750 g.)
1/4 lb. Salt Goose, Smoked Sausage or Soup Bones (optional)
1/4 lb. Pork Fat or Bacon, cut in dices (125 g.)
1/4 Tsp. Dried Sage (2 ml.)
8 Cups Beef Bouillon (2 L.)
1 Large Onion, minced (1)
1 Bay Leaf (1)
1 Tbsp. Flour, more or less (15 ml.)
Croutons, as needed

Soak peas and beans overnight. Drain and add hot water and simmer for 1 hour. Put in ham and other meat, if using any, and continue to simmer until the water is almost evaporated. In a frying pan, render the fat, remove the dices of fat and sauté the onion in the rendered fat until translucent. Incorporate flour until the fat is absorbed. While stirring constantly, gradually add l cup bouillon to make a smooth sauce or fricassee. Simmer 10 minutes. Add the fricasseed onion to the peas and beans along with the rest of the bouillon. Add the bay leaf and sage, adjust for seasonings, and simmer 30 minutes. Serve with croutons or soup breads.
Serves 8.

HACHETTE OF ALL KINDS OF MEAT

1 lb. Cooked Meat (left over roast or chicken)(500 g.)
1 Tbsp. Parsley, minced (15 ml.)
1 Shallot, Chopped (1)
1 Tsp. Dried Parsley (5 ml.)
1/4 Cup Green Onion (50 ml.)
1/4 Cup Mushroom, minced (50 ml.)
1/2 Cup Beef Bouillon (125 ml.)
3/4 Cup Soft Bread Crumbs (175 ml.)
Vinegar or Lemon Juice (few drops)

Grind or mince the meat (whatever is at hand). Place in a pot with the parsley, green onion, shallot, mushrooms and bouillon. Season with salt and pepper. Simmer covered for 15 minutes. Ladle the stock from the mixture into a baking pan. Add half the bread crumbs, then arrange the meat on top. Spread the remaining bread crumbs over meat. Put under broiler and broil until nicely browned. Sprinkle with a few drops of vinegar or lemon juice.
Serves 4.

CARROTS au BEURRE

6 Medium Sized Carrots (6)
1 Tbsp. Butter (15 ml.)
Salt and Pepper, as needed
1 Tbsp. Parsley, chopped (15 ml.)

Peel carrots and cut in thin strips. Bring water to a boil. Add carrots and cook until tender. Drain. Season with butter, salt and pepper. Toss in parsley just before serving.

BREAD PUDDING

4 Cups Bread, diced (1 L.)
1 Quart Boiling Milk (1 L.)
1 Cup Sugar (250 ml.)
6 Eggs, separated (6)
Salt, if desired
1 - 2 Tsp. Orange Flavoured Water (5 - 10 ml.)
1 Tbsp. Candied Lemon Peel, finely chopped (15 ml.)

To the bread in a bowl, add the boiling milk, sugar, salt, lemon peel and orange flavoured water. Let soak for 20 - 30 minutes. Rub through a sieve, then add the beaten egg yolks. Beat the egg whites until stiff and fold in carefully. Pour mixture in a buttered 2 quart (2.5 L.) mould or individual moulds and place in a bain marie (water bath). Bake in a 350°F (180°C) oven approximately one hour or until an inserted knife blade comes out clean. If desired, sprinkle the top with granulated sugar and broil under the broiler until golden brown. Serve with caramel sauce.
Serves 8

CARAMEL SAUCE

3 Cups Brown Sugar (750 ml.)
1/2 Cup Water (125 ml.)
1Tsp. Butter (5 ml.)
1/2 Tsp. Vanilla (2ml.)

Combine all ingredients in a saucepan. Bring to a boil, reduce heat to simmer and cook for 10 - 15 minutes.

ACADIAN

Collected by YVONNE LEVERT

CHICKEN FRICOT

1 4-5 lb. Chicken (2-3 kg.)
1/2 lb. Salt Pork (250 g.)
2 Large Onions, chopped
6 Large Potatoes, peeled and diced
2 Medium Carrots, peeled and diced
2 Tbsp. Flour (30 ml.)
3 Qts. Boiling Water (3 L.)
1 Tbsp. Salt (15 ml.)
1 Tsp. Pepper (5 ml.)
1 Tbsp. Summer Savory (15 ml.)

Cut the chicken into serving pieces. Score the salt pork into small squares and melt in a heated skillet. Fry chicken in salt pork fat until golden brown, turning pieces frequently. Remove chicken pieces from skillet and saute onion for 1 min. Add the flour and sauté for an additional 1 - 2 minutes. Place chicken pieces and onion in large pot. Add water, potatoes, carrots, salt, pepper and summer savory. Bring to a boil. Reduce heat to simmer and cook for 1 hour or until chicken is tender. Taste and adjust seasonings. *Serves 8.*

PEA SOUP

1 lb. Whole Yellow Peas (500 ml.)
4 Medium Onions, chopped
1 Tbsp. Salt (15 ml.)
1 Tsp. Black Pepper (5 ml.)
2 Qts. Cold Water (2 L.)
1/2 lb. Salt Pork, cut in half-inch cubes (250 ml.)
or Ham Bone
2 Stalks Celery, chopped

Put all ingredients in a large cooking pot, stir to combine well. Bring to a boil at high heat, reduce heat and allow to simmer for 2 - 3 hours, stirring occasionally.
Do not allow soup to stick. When done, soup will be creamy. Taste and adjust seasonings if necessary.
The soup can be served with the cubed pork, or it can be removed before service, as you wish.
If using ham bone, remove ham from bone and serve it along with the soup. *Serves 8.*

Prepared by Yvonne LeVert

GREENS WITH SWEET CREAM DRESSING

(A simple way the Acadians served
fresh garden salad)

1 Large Bunch Curly Lettuce
DRESSING:

1/2 cup Cream (125 ml.)
2 Tsp. Sugar (10 ml.)
2 Tbsp. Vinegar (30 ml.)
Salt and Pepper

Combine cream, sugar, vinegar, salt and pepper.
Whisk well. Break up fresh greens, pour on dressing
and toss salad and serve.
Note: Fresh green onions or chives can be added to salad.

ACADIAN MEAT PIE

2 lbs. Pork Shoulder, cubed (1 kg.)
2 lbs. Rabbit or Chicken (1 kg.)
2 Large Onion, chopped
1 Tbsp. Salt (15 ml.)
1 Tsp. Black Pepper (10 ml.)
2 Tbsp. Summer Savory (30 ml.)
Cold Water (as needed)

In a large pot combine cubed pork and cut up rabbit or
chicken. Add onions, salt and pepper and just enough cold
water to cover ingredients. Bring to a boil. Reduce heat and
simmer and cook uncovered for 1 hour. Add the savory and
continue cooking until meat is tender (falls away from the
bones). If mixture gets too dry, add additional water. Cool
mixture completely. Remove bones carefully. Cut the meat
into small pieces (do not remove the fat as this gives the
flavour and adds moisture).
Taste to adjust seasoning. Use to make Acadian Meat Pie.

RICH MEAT PIE PASTRY

6 Cups Flour (1.5 kg.)
2 Tbsp. Baking Powder (30 ml.)
2 Tsp. Salt (10 ml.)
2 1/2 Cups Lard (625 ml.)
2 Cups Milk (500 ml.)
1 Egg

Measure the dry ingredients in a large bowl. Carefully blend
in the lard with pastry blender or fingertips until mealy.
Gradually add the milk until dough is pliable and can be
kneaded. Kneed dough for 1 - 2 minutes. Divide the dough
into 6 pieces. Roll the pastry to 1/4 inch (6 mm.) thickness.
Line the bottom of 3 pie plates. Fill the pastry shells with
meat mixture. Cover each with top crust, flute edges and
trim excess dough. Prick the top to allow steam to escape.
Brush with egg wash (whisk egg and brush on with pastry
brush). Bake in a 400°F (200°C) oven for 25 - 30 minutes or
until crust has browned. Makes 3 - 8 inch (20 cm.) pies.
Note: Pastry trimmings can be used to decorate the pies.
To re-heat, wrap loosely in foil and place in a 300° F oven for
20 - 25 minutes.

STEWED RABBIT IN WINE

1 Large Rabbit, cut in pieces
1 Onion, finely chopped
1 Bay Leaf
1 Tsp. Savory (5 ml.)
1 Tsp. Salt (5 ml.)
1/4 Tsp. Black Pepper (1 ml.)
1 Cup Red Wine (250 ml.)
1 Cup Water (250 ml.)
1/4 Cup Butter (50 ml.)
2 Tbsp. Flour (30 ml.)

Place cut-up rabbit pieces in bowl. Combine onion, bay leaf,
savory, salt, pepper, wine and water. Pour marinade over
rabbit and allow to sit for 24 hours in refrigerator.
Occasionally stir the meat in the marinade. Remove meat
from marinade. Sponge off excessive liquid. Heat butter in
skillet until foaming. Sauté meat in butter until well browned
(reserve butter in skillet). Place meat and marinade in a
heavy casserole (add water if necessary to cover meat).
Cover. Place casserole in a 350°F (180°C) oven and cook for
one hour or until meat is tender. Remove meat pieces from
stock in casserole.
Set aside. Heat butter in skillet. Add flour and cook well
together. Add liquid from meat and cook until thickened.
Return meat to sauce and re-heat to serve.
Serves 4-6.

Note: Rabbit Stew is best served with root vegetables, carrots,
turnip, parsnip and potatoes.

HEAD CHEESE

4 lbs. Pork Shoulder (2 Kg.)
1 lb. Pork Fat (500 g.)
4 Large Onion, chopped finely
2 Large Cloves Garlic, minced
2 Tsp. Salt (10 ml.)
1 Tsp. Black Pepper (5 ml.)
2 Tsp. Summer Savory (10 ml.)
5 Whole Cloves
1/2 Tsp. Allspice (2 ml.)
6 Cups Cold Water (1.5 L.)

Cut pork shoulder and fresh pork into 3 inch pieces.
Place in heavy bottomed cooking pot. Add onion, garlic, salt,
pepper, savory, cloves, allspice and water. Cover and place
on heat and bring to a boil. Reduce to simmer and cook until
meat completely falls from bone, approximately 1 - 2 hours.
Discard bones and continue to cook uncovered until mixture
becomes thick and water has partially evaporated.
Stir occasionally. Taste mixture and add additional
seasoning if necessary. Mix well. Pour mixture into buttered
moulds and chill. Store in refrigerator. Makes a 2 pound
(1 kg.) mould. If desired use several smaller moulds.
Head Cheese freezes well. (This wonderful delicacy was first
made with a pig's head. I have worked out a much simpler
version that is delicious).

ACADIAN CRISP FRIED TROUT

6 Small Trout, cleaned and split
1 Cup Milk (250 ml.)
1 Cup Cornmeal (250 ml.)
1/2 Tsp. Pepper (2 ml.)
1/4 Tsp. Salt (1 ml.)
1/2 Tsp. Summer Savory (2 ml.)
2 Tbsp. Oil (30 ml.)
2 Tbsp. Butter (30 ml.)
Lemon Wedges

Combine cornmeal, pepper, salt and savory. Dip trout in milk then roll and coat with cornmeal mixture. Heat oil and butter in skillet. Sauté trout in fat until crisp and brown turning over to brown other side. Arrange on hot platter. Garnish with lemon wedges.

Note: Smelts can be prepared this way as well.

WHOLE WHEAT BREAD

1 Cup Warm Water (250 ml.)
2 Tsp. Sugar (10 ml.)
2 1/2 Cups Warm Milk (625 ml.)
3 Tbsp. Active Dry Yeast (45 ml.)
2 1/2 Cups White Flour (625 ml.)
3 1/2 Cups Whole Wheat Flour (875 ml.)
1 Tbsp. Salt (15 ml.)
1/2 Cup Vegetable Oil (125 ml.)

In a small bowl put water, add sugar and sprinkle in the yeast. Mix and allow to sit for 5 minutes. Scald milk and cool. Add yeast mixture to cooled milk with oil. Mix well. Combine white and whole wheat flour in a large bowl with salt. Make a well in the center, pour in the liquid mixture. Mix well and form into a ball. Kneed dough for 5 minutes on a floured board until dough is smooth and elastic. (If dough is too soft, sprinkle with additional flour while kneading.) Cover dough and let rise until double in size, 30 - 45 minutes. Punch down and shape into 2 loaves. Place in greased 9 x 5 x 3 inch (23 x 12 x7 cm.) loaf pans. Cover and let rise again approximately 30 minutes. Bake in a 400°F (200°C) oven 30 - 35 minutes or until loaf sounds hollow when tapped.

LEFT: St. Peters Church, Cheticamp   ABOVE: Les Trois Pignons, Cheticamp

ABOVE: Cheticamp

CRANBERRY APPLE TART

1 Cup Cranberries, coarsely chopped (250 ml.)
2 Cups Apples, peeled, diced (500 ml.)
1 Cup White Sugar (250 ml.)
1 Cup Cold Water (250 ml.)
2 Tbsp. Butter (30 ml.)
1/2 Cup Raisins (optional) (125 ml.)

PASTRY:

2 1/2 cups Flour (625 ml.)
3/4 Cup Shortening (175 ml.)
1/4 Cup Butter (50 ml.)
1 Tsp. Salt (5 ml.)
1/2 Cup Cold Water, approx. (125 ml.)
1 Egg, for glaze

Combine cranberries, apples, sugar, cold water and butter in medium sized saucepan. Mix well. Bring to a boil, reduce and simmer until fruit are soft and tender. Remove from heat, add raisins if desired. Cool mixture completely.

To prepare pastry, combine flour, salt, shortening and butter in a bowl using a pastry blender. Work fat into flour mixture until mixture is like coarse meal. Add water a little at a time mixing with a fork. Gather mixture into a ball. Chill for 30 minutes. Divide dough in half, roll out on a floured surface. Line a 10 inch (25 cm.) pie tin. Spread cooled filling over pastry. Roll out remaining pastry and cut into strips. Arrange strips over filling in a lattice design. Trim and flute edges. Brush strips with egg to glaze. Bake in a 375°F (190°C) oven for 25 - 30 minutes or until golden brown. Remove from oven, cool and garnish edge with whipped cream if desired. *Makes 8 servings.*

ABOVE: Cabot Trail   OVERLEAF: Margaree

ENGLISH

Collected by MRS. BRENDA BECKETT

BROWN BETTY

4 Cups Fresh Breadcrumbs (1 L.)
1/2 Cup Melted Butter (125 ml.)
8 Large Cooking Apples, peeled and sliced
1 Cup Brown Sugar (250 ml.)
2 Tsp. Cinnamon (10 ml.)
2 Tbsp. Lemon Juice (30 ml.)

Put breadcrumbs in a bowl and add melted butter mixing lightly with fork. Slice peeled apples thinly. Mix with sugar, cinnamon, lemon juice. Combine well. Butter a l quart (1 L.) mould. Spread thin layer of crumbs, then a layer of apple mixture, then more crumbs, more apples and lastly a layer of crumbs. Cover with a sheet of foil. Bake in a 350°F (180°C) oven for 20 minutes. Remove foil and bake for an additional 20 minutes or until apples are tender. If desired serve hot with ice cream or pouring cream. *Serves 6 - 8.*
Note: Apples should have started to caramelize to get the full flavour.

ALMOND SOUP

1/2 Cup Ground Almonds (125 ml.)
1 Cup Milk (250 ml.)
2 Tbsp. Fresh Breadcrumbs (30 ml.)
2 Tbsp. Butter (30 ml.)
2 Tbsp. Flour (30 ml.)
4 Cups Rich Chicken Stock (1 L)
1/2 Tsp. Salt (2 ml.)
1/4 Tsp. White Pepper (1 ml.)
Pinch of Cayenne
1 Cup Cream, heated (250 ml.)
1 Tbsp. Almonds, sliced (15 ml.)
1 Tbsp. Butter (15ml.)

Put ground almonds and milk in a small saucepan. Simmer for 5 minutes. Add bread crumbs and simmer 5 more minutes. Place mixture in food processor and puree. In a saucepan melt butter. Add flour and mix well. Add the almond puree and gradually add the stock over medium heat. Bring to a boil. Reduce to simmer. Add salt, pepper and cayenne. Simmer for 10 minutes. Remove from heat. Stir in the cream and re-heat. Melt butter and fry the slivered almonds to golden. Sprinkle over each bowl of soup before serving. *Serves 6.*

BRITISH ROAST GOOSE

1 Goose, l0 lbs. (5 kg.)
1/2 Cup White Wine (125 ml.)
Salt and Pepper
1 Onion, sliced
2 Cups Water (500 ml.)

SAGE AND ONION STUFFING:
4 Tbsp. Melted Butter (60 ml.)
4 Med. Onions, chopped
1/2 Cup Celery, chopped (125 ml.)
1 Cup Mushrooms, finely chopped (250 ml.)
4 Cups Fresh Breadcrumbs (1 L.)
2 Tsp. Dried Sage (10 ml.)
1 Tsp. Salt (5 ml.)
1 Tsp. Pepper (5 ml.)
Stock to moisten

GRAVY:
2 Tbsp. Flour (30 ml.)
Pan Drippings

Melt butter in heavy skillet. Add onion, celery and mushroom. Sauté for 5 minutes until tender. Cool and add bread crumbs, sage, salt, pepper and just enough stock to moisten. Preheat oven to 425°F (220°C). Wash goose, remove giblets and season goose with salt and pepper. Fill the cavity with stuffing. (Sew up cavity or seal with skewers) Place the goose on a rack in a large roasting pan. Prick skin at random with fork to release fat that is under the skin. Pour wine and water in roasting pan, add sliced onions and roast for l hour, basting with liquid from time to time. Reduce heat to 375°F (190°C) and roast for an additional 1 1/2 hours. Continue to baste. Cover with foil for last hour of cooking. When roasted, remove to a large serving platter. Keep warm. Remove most of the fat from roasting pan. Add flour to remaining stock, whisking continuously over medium heat until mixture thickens. Taste. Adjust seasoning and strain if necessary. Pour into gravy boat and serve with roast goose.

HOT CROSS BUNS

1/2 Cup Lukewarm Water (125 ml.)
1 Tsp. Sugar (5ml.)
2 Tbsp. Dry Yeast (30 ml.)
1 Cup Milk (250 ml.)
3/4 Cup Sugar (175 ml.)
2 Tsp. Salt (10 ml.)
1/4 Cup Soft Butter (50 ml.)
2 Eggs, beaten
2 Tsp. Cinnamon (10 ml.)
1/2 Tsp. Nutmeg (2 ml.)
5 Cups Flour (1.1 L.)
1 Cup Raisins (250 ml.)
1/2 Cup Candied Fruit (125 ml.)

In a small bowl, combine lukewarm water and sugar. Sprinkle yeast on water. Let stand for 10 minutes and whisk briskly with a fork. Scald milk and pour into a large bowl. Add sugar, salt and butter. Stir until butter melts. Cool. Add yeast mixture to cooled milk mixture along with beaten eggs, cinnamon, nutmeg. Combine flour with raisins and fruit. Coat fruit well with flour. Add flour to liquid mixture 2 cups at a time. Mix well after each addition. Work in the last of the flour mixture with a rotary motion of the hand. Turn dough onto a lightly floured surface and kneed for 8 - 10 minutes. (Dough should be pliable but not sticky). Shape into a smooth ball and place in a greased bowl. Cover and let rise to double about 1 - 1 1/2 hours. Punch down and shape into 18 - 20 buns. Arrange 2 inches apart on greased baking sheet. Cover and let rise until doubled, about 35 - 40 minutes. Before baking brush buns with a mixture of 1 egg white, 1 Tbsp. (15 ml.) water. whisked together. Slash top of bun to form a cross. Bake in preheated 400°F (200°C) oven for 15 - 18 minutes. *Makes 18 - 20 buns.*

TOP: Baddeck   ABOVE: Englishtown Ferry

20

ROAST PRIME RIB OF BEEF/YORKSHIRE PUDDING

4 lbs. Prime Rib (2 Kg.)
2 Tbsp. Butter (30 ml.)
1 Tbsp. Oil (15 ml.)
Salt and Pepper to Season
1 Cup Beef Stock (250 ml.)

Preheat oven to 325°F (160°C). Place beef in a roasting pan. Brush with oil and dot with butter. Sprinkle with salt and pepper. Put in oven and baste occasionally 1 1/4 hours for rare and 1 1/2 hours for medium (or use meat thermometer). Remove from oven and allow to settle for 20 minutes before carving.

TO MAKE GRAVY:
Skim some of the fat from pan juices. Add stock and boil scraping pan to deglaze. Reduce on medium heat for 8 - 10 minutes. Season with salt and pepper, strain and serve.

YORKSHIRE PUDDING

2 Tbsp. Beef Drippings or Oil (30 ml.)
1 Cup Flour (250 ml.)
2 Eggs
1 Cup Milk (260 ml.)
1/2 Tsp. Salt (2 ml.)
1 Tbsp. Oil (15 ml.)

Combine eggs and milk in a small bowl of electric mixer. Beat at lowest speed for 1 minute. Add flour 1/2 cup (125 ml.) at a time blending well after each addition. Add salt and 1 tbsp. of oil (15 ml.). Beat at high speed of mixer for 5 minutes. Place 1 tsp. of oil (5 ml.) in each of 12 muffin cups. Place muffin tin in 450°F (250°C) oven for 5 minutes. Pour batter in sizzling muffin cups. Bake 450°F (230°C) for 20 minutes. Reduce temperature to 350°F(180°C) and bake an additional 10 minutes. Remove from oven and serve with roast beef.

Note: Yorkshire pudding can also be made in a baking pan and cut in squares to serve.

Prepared by Chef Craig Vincent, Joe's Warehouse, Sydney

21

SCOTTISH

Collected by
MRS. MARY MACKEIGAN
and MRS. MARY MUIR

SCOTCH BROTH

2 lbs. Beef Shank (500 ml.)
3 Tbsp. Butter (45ml.)
3 Onions, sliced (3)
3 Carrots, diced (3)
2 Stocks Celery, diced (2)
3 Potatoes, diced (3)
1/2 Cup Pearl Barley (125 ml.)
2 Tsp. Salt (10 ml.)
1 Tsp. Black Pepper (5ml.)
8 Cups Water (2 L.)

Place beef shank in roaster pan in a 450°F (230°C) oven for 30 minutes or until shank is completely browned. Remove from oven and place in a large soup pot. Cover with water and bring to a boil. Simmer for 1 hour. Melt butter in skillet and sauté onions, carrots and celery for 5 minutes or until softened. Add vegetables to beef shank with diced potatoes, barley, salt and pepper. Simmer for 1 hour or until vegetables are tender and soup is thick. Taste to adjust seasoning.
Serves 6 - 8.

MARAGHAN

2 Cups Regular Rolled Oats (500 ml.)
1 1/2 Cups Beef Suet, ground (375 ml.)
1 Cup Onion, chopped (250 ml.)
1 Tbsp. Salt (15ml.)
1 Tsp. Black Pepper (10 ml.)

Combine rolled oats, suet, salt and pepper. Mix together, add onion, combining well. Cover and refrigerate overnight. (Purchase beef casing from butcher.) Fill casing with cold water. (this will stretch casing). Tie a string around the bottom. Leave filled with water overnight. Place large funnel over casing and fill, packing the mixture well. Tie securely and pierce casing several times with a fork. Place Maraghan in a pot of boiling salted water. Cook for approximately 35 minutes, piercing casing from time to time. Remove from water and drain. Maraghan is delicious served with boiled potato and sliced cooked turnip.
Serves 4.

ABOVE: Nova Scotia Highland Village, Iona   RIGHT: Mother of Seven Sorrows Shrine, Mabou

STOVIES

4 Medium Potatoes (4)
2 Medium Onions (2)
3 Tbsp. Bacon Fat or Butter, melted (45 ml.)
1 Tsp. Salt (5 ml.)
1/2 Tsp. Pepper (2 ml.)
1 Cup Water (250 ml.)
1 Tbsp. Parsley, chopped (15 ml.)

Peel and slice potatoes and onions. Place in alternate layers in a buttered skillet. Season well with salt and pepper. Pour over melted fat and water. Cook covered for 15 - 20 minutes at medium heat or until tender and most of the liquid is absorbed. (Shake skillet occasionally to avoid sticking). To serve sprinkle with parsley. *Serves 4.*

SCOTTISH PANCAKES

2 cups flour (500 ml.)
1/4 Tsp. Salt (1 ml.)
1 Tsp. Baking Soda (5 ml.)
1 1/2 Tsp. Cream of Tartar (7 ml.)
1/2 Cup Granulated Sugar (125 ml.)
2 Eggs, lightly beaten (2)
1/2 Cup Margarine, melted (125 ml.)
1 Cup Milk (250 ml.)

In a bowl combine flour, salt, baking soda, cream of tartar and sugar. Make a well in the center and add the lightly beaten eggs. Add the melted margarine slowly to eggs and gradually work the flour into the mixture beating well to avoid lumps. Add the milk a little at a time beating well after each addition. The mixture should be smooth and thick. To cook pancakes, lightly grease the bottom of a heavy fry pan, or electric skillet, heat pan and drop one tsp. of mixture in the pan. Mixture should spread to 2 inches (5 cm.).
Cook until golden on each side. Place on rack to cool. Scottish Pancakes are like a sweet bread and are served with butter, preserves or marmalade.

SCOTCH EGGS

6 Eggs, hard cooked (6)
1 lb. Sausage Meat (500 g)
1 Cup Bread Crumbs (250 ml.)
2 Tbsp. Fresh Parsley, chopped (30 ml.)
1/2 Tsp. Summer Savory (2 ml.)
1/4 Tsp. Black Pepper (1 ml.)
1 Egg (1)

Peel eggs and wrap each in sausage meat making sure eggs are evenly coated. Combine bread crumbs with parsley, savory and pepper. In a small bowl lightly beat egg with a fork. Dip sausage coated eggs in egg mixture and roll in crumb mixture. Coat eggs well with crumbs. Chill for one hour if time allows. Place eggs on a lightly greased baking sheet and bake for 30 - 35 minutes in a 375°F (190 °C) oven until coating is crisp and browned. Turn several times during baking process. Serve hot or cold. *NOTE: To use as appetizers, cut each egg in half lengthwise and accompany with hot mustard. Scotch Eggs can also be deep fried.*

RIGHT: Nova Scotia Highland Village, Iona

SMOKED FISH PIE

1/2 lb. Smoked Haddock or Salt Cod (250 g.)
1 lb. Fresh Haddock (500 g.)
1 Cup Milk (250 ml.)
2 Tbsp. Water (30 ml.)
1 Bay leaf
1 Medium Onion, chopped
2 Tbsp. Butter (30 ml.)
2 Tbsp. Flour (30 ml.)
1/4 Cup Cheddar Cheese, grated (50 ml.)
2 Eggs, hard boiled
1 Tsp. Salt (5 m.)
1/2 Tsp. Pepper (2 ml.)
5 Large Potatoes
1/2 Cup Hot Milk (125 ml.)
4 Tbsp. Butter (60 ml.)
Salt and Pepper
2 Tbsp. Butter (30 ml.)

Put both fish in a baking dish and cover with milk. Add bay leaf. Bake uncovered in a 350°F (180°C) oven for 20 minutes. Remove from oven. Cool enough to handle. Skin and flake the fish in large flakes. Strain the cooking liquid and set aside. Melt butter and sauté chopped onion. Add flour and cook stirring one minute. Add the milk from the fish; bring to a boil. Reduce heat and cook until thickened. Fold in the grated cheese, flaked fish and coarsely chopped eggs, parsley, salt and pepper. Taste sauce and adjust seasoning. Pour mixture into a 10 inch (1.2 L) deep baking dish. Cook potatoes in boiling, salted water until tender. Drain and mash; add hot milk and butter. Season with salt and pepper. Cover fish pie with mashed potato, form rough peaks with potato. Dot with remaining butter. Bake in a 400°F (200 °C) oven for 25 minutes until pie is lightly browned and bubbly around the edges. *Serves 6.*

POUND CAKE

1 lb. Butter (500 g.)
1 lb. Sugar (500 g.)
1 lb. Flour (500 g.)
10 Egg Whites (10)
10 Egg Yolks (10)
1/4 Tsp. Cream of Tartar (1 ml.)
1 Tsp. Salt (5 ml.)
2 Tsp. Lemon Juice (10 ml.)
1 Tsp. Almond Flavouring (5 ml.)
2 Tbsp. Rum or Water (30 ml.)

Cream the butter until it is very light. Gradually add the sugar and continue beating until sugar is dissolved in butter. (10 - 15 minutes). Add egg yolks two at a time beating continuously. Add the lemon juice, almond, rum or water. Combine flour and salt and add to creamed mixture and beat for 5 minutes. Add cream of tartar to egg whites and beat until stiff peaks form. Fold egg whites into batter. Pour batter into a well greased and paper lined tube pan. Bake in a 275°F (149°C) oven for 2 hours or until cake tester comes out clean. Remove from oven. Cool for 10 minutes. Remove from pan. Cool and store. *Note: Pound Cake should be allowed to "mellow" for 3 - 4 days before serving.*

CAPE BRETON OATCAKES

"A Cape Breton tradition that became popular throughout Canada"

3 Cups Rolled Oats (750 ml.)
2 Cups Flour (500 ml.)
1 Cup White Sugar (250 ml.)
1 Tsp. Salt (5 ml.)
1 Tsp. Soda (5 ml.)
1 1/2 Cups Shortening (375 ml.)
6 Tbsp. Cold Water (90 ml.)

Stir rolled oats, flour, sugar, salt and soda in a bowl.
Work in shortening with fingertips until crumbly.
Sprinkle with water, form in a ball with your hands.
Roll out fairly thin on a floured surface. Cut in 2 1/2 inch (6 cm.) squares or circles. Arrange on lightly greased cookie sheet. Bake 375°F (190°C) oven approximately 10 - 15 minutes until lightly browned.
Makes 3 dozen Oatcakes.

IRISH

Collected by MRS. FLORA FITZGERALD

IRISH STEW

4 lbs. Boneless Stewing Lamb (2 kg.)
4 Medium Onions, sliced (4)
2 Whole Cloves Garlic (2)
1 Bay Leaf (1)
1 Tbsp. Salt (15ml.)
2 Tsp. Pepper (10 ml.)
8 Medium Potatoes, peeled and quartered (8)
1 Quart Water (1 L.)

Cut lamb in 2 inch (5 cm.) pieces. Arrange meat and potatoes in a casserole in layers starting and finishing with potatoes. Season well between each layer with salt and pepper. Add bay leaf, garlic cloves and water. Cover tightly and cook in a 325°F (180°C) oven for 2 1/2 hours or until meat is very tender and gravy is rich and thick. Avoid stirring but shake the casserole from time to time to avoid sticking. *Serves 6.*

IRISH COFFEE

1 1/4 oz. Irish Whiskey (40 ml.)
1 Cup Hot Strong Black Coffee (250 ml.)
1 1/2 Tsp. Brown Sugar (7 ml.)
1 Tbsp. Whipping Cream (15 ml.)

Pour Irish Whiskey and black coffee into a warmed stem glass. Add sugar and stir well. Carefully pour the whipping cream over the back of a spoon, holding spoon at the edge of the glass. Remove spoon gently. Do not mix the cream through the coffee. The hot whiskey laced coffee is sipped through the velvety cream. *Yield: 1 serving.*

ABOVE: Irish Cove

IRISH COFFEE BREAD

2 Cups Flour (500 ml.)
2 Cups Whole Wheat Flour (500 ml.)
2 Tbsp. Granulated Sugar (30 ml.)
2 Tsp. Baking Powder (10 ml.)
1 1/2 Tsp. Baking Soda (7 ml.)
1 Tsp. Salt (5 ml.)
2 Tbsp. Butter (30 ml.)
1 3/4 Cups Milk (425 ml.)
2 Tbsp. Vinegar (30 ml.)

Mix vinegar and milk. Set aside. Combine flour, sugar, baking powder, baking soda and salt. Cut in butter until mixture is crumbly. Add milk and stir to make a soft dough. Turn out onto lightly floured counter and knead about 10 times until smooth. Flatten dough into a circle about 2 1/2 inches thick. Place on greased baking sheet and cut a large cross on top. Bake 1 hour 400 °F oven (200°C) or until a toothpick inserted in the centre comes out clean.

IRISH SODA BREAD

3/4 Cup Raisins (175 ml.)
2 Cups Flour (500 ml.)
1 Tbsp. Sugar (15 ml.)
2 Tsp. Baking Powder (10 ml.)
1 Tsp. Salt (5 ml.)
1/2 Tsp. Baking Soda (2 ml.)
1/3 Cup Shortening (75 ml.)
1 Tsp. Caraway Seed (Optional) (5 ml.)
1 Egg (1)
1 Cup Sour Milk (250 ml.)

Rinse raisins in hot water. Drain and pat dry. Sift flour, sugar, baking powder, salt and soda into a medium sized mixing bowl. With two knives or a hand blender, cut in shortening until mixture is the texture of coarse meal. Stir in caraway seed and raisins. Combine egg and sour milk, whisk together. Stir egg mixture into flour mixture. Mix only enough to dampen flour. (do not over mix) Grease a 8 inch (20 x 20 cm.) baking pan. Spread mixture in pan. Make a cross in center of dough. Bake in a 400°F (200°C) oven for 30 minutes or until done. Serve with butter.
Note: To make sourmilk add 1 Tbsp. (15 ml.) vinegar to 1 Cup (250 ml.) milk. Mix well and let sit for 5 minutes.

ABOVE: Margaree OVERLEAF: Mabou Harbour

27

TRADITIONAL

Collected by YVONNE LEVERT

Soups, Salads & Appetizers

CLAM CHOWDER

1 Quart Shucked Clams (1 L.)
1/4 Cup Cubed Salt Pork (50 ml.)
1 Cup Onion, diced (250 ml.)
4 Cups Raw Potatoes, diced (1 L.)
2 Cups Boiling Water (500 ml.)
2 Cups Milk, heated (500 ml.)
1 Cup Light Cream, heated (250 ml.)
1 Tsp. Salt (5 ml.)
Pepper, freshly ground

If using fresh clams, shuck and reserve clams and liquid.
Fry the salt pork until crisp. Sauté the onion in rendered fat.
Place in a large saucepan. Combine potatoes with onion and
pork. Cover with boiling water. Add clams and liquid.
Bring to a boil and simmer until potatoes are tender.
Add milk, cream, salt and pepper and simmer for 10 minutes.
Do not boil.
Serves 6.

LOBSTER CHOWDER

1 Large Onion, chopped
4 Tbsp. Butter (60 ml.)
4 Large Potatoes, peeled and diced
2 Cups Hot Water (500 ml.)
3 Cups Lobster Meat, cut in chunks (750 ml.)
4 Tbsp. Butter (60 ml.)
1 Tsp. Salt (5 ml.)
1/2 Tsp. Pepper (2 ml.)
1/4 Tsp. Thyme (1 ml.)
2 Tbsp. Parsley, freshly chopped (30 ml.)
2 Cups Light Cream, heated (500 ml.)
2 Cups Milk, heated (500 ml.)

In a deep skillet melt the butter and sauté onion until tender.
Add potatoes, water, salt, pepper, thyme and parsley. Bring
to a boil Turn down heat and simmer for approximately 15
minutes until potatoes are tender. Sauté lobster in additional
butter and add to potato mixture. Carefully add heated milk
and cream. Combine well. Re-heat but do not boil.
Serves 8.

FISH CHOWDER

2 lbs. Haddock or Cod Fillets (1 kg.)
1/4 lb. Salt Pork, diced (125 g.)
1 Large Onion, diced
2 Cups Boiling Water (500 ml.)
1 Tsp. Salt (5 ml.)
1/4 Tsp. Pepper (1 ml.)
3 Cups Milk (750 ml.)
1 Cup Cream (250 ml.)
1 Tbsp. Butter (15 ml.)
1 Tbsp. Green Onion, chopped (15 ml.)

Sauté pork until crisp, add onion and sauté for another few minutes. Add boiling water and potatoes and cook until potatoes are tender. Cut fish fillets in 2 - 3 inch pieces. Add fish to potatoes and simmer until fish flakes, about 5 - 6 minutes. Combine milk, cream and butter in a saucepan and heat to scald milk. Do not boil. Slowly pour hot milk mixture into the potato and fish mixture. Stir carefully to combine. Season with salt and pepper. Pour into a soup terrine and garnish with green chopped onion.
Note: Served with thick home made bread or tea biscuits, it makes a meal.

CORN CHOWDER

2 Cups Raw Potatoes, diced (500 g.)
1/2 Cup Onion, chopped (125 ml.)
4 Tbsp. Butter (60 ml.)
2 Cups Boiling Water (500 ml.)
3 Cups Creamed Corn (750 ml.)
3 Cups Milk, heated (750 ml.)
1 Tsp. Salt (5 ml.)
1 Tsp. Black Pepper (5 ml.)
1 Tsp. Thyme (5 ml.)
1 Tbsp. Fresh Parsley, chopped (15 ml.)

Peel and dice potatoes. Place in cold water until needed. Melt butter in saucepan. Sauté chopped onion until tender. Drain potatoes and toss into onion mixture. Add boiling water, salt, pepper and thyme. Simmer until potatoes are tender. Add corn and milk. Simmer for 15 minutes (do not boil). Add chopped parsley and taste to adjust seasoning. *Serves 6.*

VEGETABLE SOUP

1 Cup Carrot, diced (250 ml.)
1/2 Cup Onion, diced (125 ml.)
1 Cup Turnip, diced (250 ml.)
1 Cup Green Beans, cut into pieces (250 ml.)
1/2 Cup Potatoes, diced (125 ml.)
4 Tbsp. Butter (60 ml.)
1/2 Cup Frozen Peas
1/2 Cup Barley, rinsed in cold water (125 ml.)
2 Tsp. Salt (10 ml.)
1 Tsp. Black Pepper (5 ml.)
1 Bay Leaf
1 Tsp. Summer Savory (5 ml.)
2 Quarts Rich Stock (2 L.)

Prepare vegetables. Melt butter in large saucepan. Sauté all vegetables except peas. To the vegetables add barley, salt, pepper, bay leaf, summer savory and stock. Bring to a boil, reduce to simmer and cook for 45 minutes until barley and vegetables are tender. Add peas. Cook for 5 minutes. Taste to adjust seasoning. Serve with homemade bread. *Serves 6.*

CABBAGE SOUP

1   3 lb. Shank of Beef (1.5 Kg.)
3 Quarts Cold Water (3 L.)
1 Tbsp. Salt (15 ml.)
1 Tsp. Black Pepper (5 ml.)
1 Bay Leaf
1 Tsp. Thyme (5ml.)
1/2 Tsp. Savory (2 ml.)
1 Small Head Cabbage, chopped
2 Medium Onion, chopped
2 Medium Carrots, diced
2 Cups Diced Celery (500 ml.)

Soak the beef shank in water for 2 hours. Place in a large cooking pot. Add the bay leaf, salt, pepper, thyme and savory. Bring to a boil and reduce heat. Simmer for 2 - 3 hours (remove scum from stock as if forms). Remove the shank, add cabbage, onion, carrots and celery. Simmer until vegetables are tender. Taste and adjust seasoning. *Serves 8.*

ISLAND STEAMED MUSSELS

5 lbs. Mussels in shell (2.5 kg.)
1 Medium Onion, chopped
1 Tsp. Black Pepper (5 ml.)
1 Cup White Wine or Water (250 ml.)
4 Tbsp. Chopped Parsley (60 ml.)
4 Tbsp. Butter (60 ml.)
Lemon Juice, as needed

Scrub mussels with a stiff brush. Scrape to remove beards. Place the mussels in a large cooking pot. Add onions, pepper, white wine and parsley. Cover pot and bring to a boil. Cook until mussels open, approximately 5 minutes. Remove mussels from liquid (discard unopened mussels). Strain liquid. Melt butter in small saucepan. Add strained liquid and lemon juice as needed. Place mussels in large soup bowls and place sauce in dipping bowls. *Serves 4 - 6.*

BAKED OYSTERS ON THE HALF SHELL

12 Oysters, shucked
1/2 cup Mushrooms, finely chopped (125 ml.)
1 Bunch Green Onion, chopped
1 Clove Garlic, crushed
2 Tbsp. Butter (30 ml.)
1 Cup Fresh Breadcrumbs (250 ml.)
1/2 Tsp. Salt (2 ml.)
1/4 Tsp. Pepper (1 ml.)
1/2 Tsp. Dill Weed (2ml.)
6 Tbsp. Cream (90 ml.)
6 Tbsp. Oyster Juice (90 ml.)
1/2 Cup Swiss Cheese, grated (125 ml.)

Wash and lightly butter 12 oyster shells. Sauté mushrooms, onion and garlic in butter. Combine breadcrumbs, salt, pepper and dill. Mix well. Place an oyster in each shell. Combine cream and oyster juice and heat. Pour 1 tbsp. (30 ml.) over each oyster. Divide bread mixture over oysters. Sprinkle with grated cheese. Bake in a 375°F (190°C) oven for 15 - 20 minutes. Serve as an appetizer.

TO OPEN OYSTERS: Hold the shell with deep half down in a towel. Insert the oyster knife between the shells near the hinge and twist apart. Retain the juice and strain.

HOT CRAB CANAPE

1 Cup Cooked Crab, flaked (250 ml.)
1/2 Cup Celery, finely chopped (125 ml.)
1/4 Cup Red Pepper, finely chopped (50 ml.)
2 Green Onions, finely chopped
1/2 Tsp. Black Pepper (2 ml.)
1/2 Cup Mayonnaise (125 ml.)
1/4 Cup Cheddar Cheese, grated (50 ml.)

Combine crab, celery, red pepper, green onion, pepper and mayonnaise. Spread mixture on the rounds of toast. Place on baking sheet. Sprinkle with cheese and broil for l minute. *Makes 8 - 12 servings.*

CRAB MEAT SALAD

2 Cups Crab Meat (500 ml.)
2 Green Onions, chopped
1 Cup Celery, chopped (250 g.)
1/2 Cup Red Pepper, chopped (125 ml.)
2 Tbsp. Pimento, chopped (30 ml.)
4 Hard Cooked Eggs, chopped
1/2 Tsp. Salt (2 ml.)
Pepper, freshl;y ground
Pinch of Cayenne Pepper
3/4 Cup Mayonnaise (175 ml.)
Lettuce Leaves

Place crab meat in a bowl. Do not break up. To crab add onion, celery, red pepper, pimento, eggs, salt, pepper and cayenne. Carefully fold in the mayonnaise. Chill. Serve on crisp leaves of lettuce.
Serves 6.

EYKING FARM LAYERED VEGETABLE SALAD

1 Medium Head Iceberg Lettuce
1 Cup Celery, diced (250 ml.)
1 Cup Red Pepper, diced (250 ml.)
1/2 Cup Green Pepper, diced (125 ml.)
1 Cup Green Onion, chopped (250 ml.)
2 Cups Frozen Peas (500 ml.)
5 Hard Cooked Eggs, sliced
1 1/2 Cups Mayonnaise (375 ml.)
2 Tbsp. Wine Vinegar (30 ml.)
1/2 Tsp. Basil (2 ml.)
1 Tbsp. Granulated Sugar (15 ml.)
1 Tsp. Ground Pepper, freshly (5 ml.)
1/2 Tsp. Salt (2 ml.)
1 Large Garlic Clove, crushed
6 Slices Crisp, cooked bacon in bite size pieces
1 Cup Mozzarella or Swiss Cheese, grated (250 ml.)
2 Tbsp. Parsley, chopped (30 ml.)

In a large, deep glass bowl layer lettuce, celery, red pepper, green pepper, onion, peas and eggs. Combine mayonnaise, wine vinegar, basil, sugar, pepper, salt and crushed garlic. Spread evenly over bowl of vegetables spreading dressing around the edge. Cover and refrigerate for several hours or overnight. Shortly before serving, cook bacon and spread warm over salad. Sprinkle with cheese and garnish with chopped parsley.

BAKED BEANS

2 lbs. Yellow Eyed Beans (1 Kg.)
1/2 Cup Salt Pork, diced (125 ml.)
1 Small Onion, chopped (1)
1/2 Cup Brown Sugar, packed (125 ml.)
1/2 Cup Molasses (125 ml.)
4 Tbsp. Chili Sauce (60 ml.)
2 Tsp. Dry Mustard (10 ml.)
1 Tsp. Salt (5 ml.)
1 Tsp. Black Pepper (5 ml.)

Rinse and sort beans. Soak overnight in cold water. Place beans in a saucepan. Bring to a boil and cook until skins split (5 - 10 minutes). Drain beans, reserve liquid and place in bean crock or casserole. Add onion, salt pork, mustard, salt, pepper and reserved liquid to completely cover the beans. Cover and bake in a 275°F (140°C) oven for 2 1/2 hours. Combine molasses, brown sugar and chili sauce. Carefully fold mixture into beans. Cover and bake for 1 hour in a 375°F (190°C) oven until beans are tender. *Serves 10 - 12.*

NOTE: If beans become too dry, add additional reserved liquid.

ABOVE: Nova Scotia Highland Village, Iona.   OVERLEAF: Low Point Light.

Vegetables

HODGE PODGE

12 Baby Carrots
1 Small Turnip, thinly sliced
1 Cup Green Peas (250 ml.)
2 Cups Green Beans (500 ml.)
5 Medium Potatoes, sliced
1 Large Onion, sliced
4 Tbsp. Butter, melted (60 ml.)
1 Cup Light Cream (250 ml.)
1 Tsp. Salt (5 ml.)
1/2 Tsp. Pepper (2 ml.)
1/2 Tsp. Summer Savory (2 ml.)

In a large saucepan put carrots, turnip and potato. Cover with water. Bring to a boil and partially cook. Add prepared beans, peas and onion. Cook until all are tender. Drain vegetables and arrange in a greased casserole. Combine melted butter, cream and savory. Pour over vegetables. Season with salt and pepper. Cover and bake in a 300°F (150°C) oven for 30 minutes or until vegetables are tende.
Serves 6.

PARSNIP PATTIES

1 lb Parsnip (500 g.)
2 Tbsp. Butter (30 ml.)
1 Tsp. Salt (5 ml.)
1/2 Tsp. Pepper (2 ml.)
1/2 Cup Flour (125 ml.)
4 Tbsp. Butter (60 ml.)

Peel parsnip. Cut in pieces. Place in saucepan. Cover with water. Cook until parsnips are tender. Drain parsnips. Mash to a pulp. Add 2 tbsp. butter, salt and pepper. Cool and shape mixture into small flat cakes. Roll cakes in flour. Chill for 15 minutes. Melt and heat remaining butter. Add parsnip cakes and fry to a golden brown on each side. Serve as a vegetable.
Serves 4 - 6.

Seafood

SIMPLE BAKED SCALLOPS

1 lb. Fresh Scallops (500 g.)
1 Cup Fresh Bread Crumbs (250 ml.)
1 Tbsp. Fresh Parsley, chopped (15 ml.)
1/2 Tsp. Dill Weed (2 ml.)
1/2 Tsp. Salt (2 ml.)
1/2 Tsp. Pepper, freshly ground (2 ml.)
1 Clove Garlic, crushed
1/4 Cup Butter, melted (50 ml.)
1 Cup Light Cream, heated (250 ml.)
1/2 Cup Swiss Cheese, grated (125 ml.)

Rinse scallops and drain well. In a bowl combine bread crumbs, parsley, dill, salt and pepper. Toss in the melted butter and crushed garlic and combine well. Sprinkle half the crumbs in bottom of a quart size (1 L.) baking dish. Distribute scallops over crumbs. Pour the heated cream over scallops. Top with remaining crumbs and sprinkle with cheese. Bake at 375°F (190°C) for approximately 20 - 25 minutes until scallops are tender. *Serves 6. Variation: Arrange in individual scallop shells and bake for 10 - 15 minutes each.*

POACHED SALMON WITH EGG SAUCE

4 lbs. Salmon (2 kg.)
1 Onion, chopped
2 Carrots, chopped
1/4 Cup Chives, chopped (50 ml.)
2 Tsp. Salt (10 ml.)
2 Quarts Cold Water (2 L)

Rinse salmon and place in a baking pan or roaster. Arrange chopped carrots, onion and chives over salmon. Sprinkle with salt. Cover salmon completely with cold water. Bring to boil, reduce heat and simmer allowing 10 minutes per pound of salmon. Salmon is cooked when it flakes with a fork. Remove salmon from cooking water. Place on serving tray and discard skin. Serve with egg sauce.

EGG SAUCE

2 Tbsp. Butter (30 ml.)
2 Tbsp. Flour (30 ml.)
2 Cups Milk, heated (500 ml.)
1/2 Tsp. Salt (2 ml.)
1/4 Tsp. Pepper (1 ml.)
Few Grains Nutmeg
2 Eggs, boiled, chopped

Melt butter in saucepan and add flour. Cook over a medium heat for 1 minute. Add hot milk, salt, pepper and nutmeg. Bring to a boil stirring constantly until sauce thickens and is smooth. Remove from heat and fold in the chopped eggs. Taste to adjust seasoning. Keep sauce warm. Serve with poached salmon. *Serves 8.*

BOILED MAIN-A-DIEU LOBSTER

In Cape Breton most people enjoy lobster served in simple ways, the most common being hot or cold served from the shell accompanied by butter, lemon juice or mayonnaise. (All of these condiments create heated discussions)

Each pound of lobster (500 g) yields approximately 1/4 pound (125 g.) cooked lobster meat.

Fill a large canning kettle with enough water to cover lobsters. Add 1/4 cup (50 ml.) salt for each quart or litre of water. Bring water to a rapid boil. Drop the live lobster head first into the water (this insures instant death). Cover the pot and cook for 20 minutes. Remove lobster from hot water and plunge them in cold salted water to prevent over cooking. Shake lobster gently to extract any excess water. Crack open and enjoy!!

COOKING TIMES:

1 - 1/2 lbs. (500 - 750 g.)	10 - 15 minutes
1 1/2 - 2 lbs. (750 g. - 1 kg)	15 - 18 minutes
2 1/2 - 5 lbs. (1.5 kg. - 2.5 kg.)	20 - 25 minutes

SMOTHERED SALMON

2 lb. Fresh Salmon (1 kg.)
1/2 Cup Butter, melted (125 ml.)
1 Cup Cold Water (250 ml.)
1 Tsp. Salt (5 ml.)
1/2 Tsp. Black Pepper (2 ml.)
1 Bunch Green Onion, chopped
8 Spinach Leaves

Arrange spinach leaves in the bottom of a heavy casserole or skillet. Place salmon on leaves. Sprinkle with salt and pepper. Carefully pour melted butter and arrange chopped onion over salmon. Cover casserole with foil. Place in a 300°F (150°C) oven and cook for approximately 25 - 30 minutes. (Baste once during cooking). Remove from oven; arrange spinach and salmon on serving platter. Baste with juices. Serve with fresh summer vegetables. *Serves 4 - 6.*

BARBECUE MACKEREL, CAPE BRETON STYLE

2 lbs. Mackerel (1 Kg.)
2 Tbsp. Butter, melted (30 ml.)
1 Tbsp. Lemon Juice (15 ml.)
Salt and Pepper

Place each serving of mackerel on a sheet of aluminum foil. Combine lemon juice and melted butter. Brush mackerel with lemon/butter mixture. Season with salt and pepper. Wrap foil around mackerel forming a packet. Have barbecue heated at medium and place packets on the grill. Allow 10 minutes time per inch thickness. Turn packets occasionally. Cook until fish is opaque. *Serves 4.*

LEMON HALIBUT WITH SOUR CREAM

2 lbs. Halibut Steaks (1 kg.)
2 Tbsp. Olive Oil (30 ml.)
2 Tbsp. Butter (30 ml.)
1 Bunch Green Onions, chopped
1 Medium Onion, chopped
3 Tbsp. Fresh Lemon Juice (45 ml.)
2 Tbsp. Lemon Rind (30 ml.)
2 Tbsp. Fresh Parsley, chopped (30 ml.)
1 Cup Sour Cream (250 ml.)
2 Tsp. Curry Powder (10 ml.)
Salt and Pepper to taste

Cut the halibut in serving size pieces. Remove bones. Heat oil and butter in large fry pan and cook the onions until transparent. Add halibut to pan. Combine lemon juice, rind, parsley, sour cream, curry powder, salt and pepper. Pour over halibut and simmer for 20 minutes basting sauce over fish occasionally. Serve hot. Serve on a bed of rice with vegetable accompaniment. *Makes 4 - 6 servings.*

PAN FRIED HADDOCK FILLETS

2 lbs. Haddock Fillets (1 kg.)
1/2 Tsp. Salt (2ml.)
1/4 Tsp. Pepper (1 ml.)
1/2 Tsp. Tarragon (2 ml.)
1/2 Cup Flour (125 ml.)
Oil for frying as needed
4 Tbsp. Lemon Juice (60 ml.)
1 Clove Garlic, crushed
2 Tbsp. Fresh Parsley, chopped (30 ml.)
5 Tbsp. Butter (75 ml.)

Cut fillets in serving size portions. Season with salt and pepper and coat well with flour. Heat oil in a skillet and pan fry in hot oil until golden brown - approximately 3 - 4 minutes on each side. Remove fish and place on heated platter. Melt butter in small saucepan. Add crushed garlic and lemon juice and tarragon. Heat until butter foams. Pour over fish fillets and serve immediately.
Makes 4 - 6 servings.

ABOVE: Green Cove

SOLE FILLETS
WITH SHRIMP STUFFING

1 lb. Sole Fillets (500 g.)
1/2 Tsp. Salt (2 ml.)
1/4 Tsp. Pepper (1 ml.)
3 Tbsp. Butter, melted (45 ml.)
2 Tbsp. Lemon Juice (30 ml.)
1 Tbsp. Fresh Parsley, chopped (15 ml.)

STUFFING:

1 Cup Cooked Shrimp (250 ml.)
1/2 Cup Celery, finely chopped (125 ml.)
1 Medium Onion, chopped
1 Tsp. Dill Weed (5 ml.)
1/2 Tsp. Pepper (2 ml.)
4 Tbsp. Butter, melted (60 ml.)

Prepare fillets by cutting into 6" x 2" (15 x 2 cm.) pieces.
Set aside. Prepare stuffing (if shrimp are large, chop).
Melt butter, cook celery and onion in butter. Toss in shrimp,
breadcrumbs, dill and pepper. Mix well. Divide stuffing
between fillets placing stuffing on wide end. Wrap fillet
around stuffing. Secure with toothpick. Place on a buttered
baking dish. Combine melted butter and lemon juice and
pour over rolls. Bake in a 450°F (230°C) oven for about
10 minutes. Garnish with chopped parsley. *Serves 6.*

NEWBURG OF FINNAN HADDIE

1 lb. Finnan Haddie Fillets (500 g.)
4 Tbsp. Butter (60 ml.)
2 Tbsp. Flour (30 ml.)
1 1/2 Cups Milk, heated (375 g.)
1/4 Tsp. Salt (1 ml.)
1/2 Tsp. Pepper (2 ml.)
1 Tsp. Paprika (5 ml.)
1 Tsp. Sherry (5 ml.)
3 Egg Yolks
1 Cup Cream (250 ml.)
1/4 Tsp. Nutmeg (1 ml.)
4 Tbsp. Parsley, chopped (60 ml.)

Flake the finnan haddie fillets and set aside. Melt butter
in saucepan. Add flour and cook stirring constantly for
1 minute. Add heated milk, salt, pepper and paprika.
Bring to a boil and cook until sauce thickens
(about 2 - 3 minutes). Remove from heat and add flaked
finnan haddie. Combine egg yolks, cream and sherry and
carefully pour into creamed mixture. Combine well.
Re-heat mixture over a low heat stirring occasionally
(do not boil). Serve with rice, in pastry shell or with toast
points. Garnish with chopped parsley.
Serves 6.

ABOVE: Seafood buffet prepared by Chef Bill King, North Star Inn, North Sydney

CODFISH AU GRATIN

2 lbs. Cooked Cod Fillets (1 kg.)
4 Tbsp. Butter (60 ml.)
4 Tbsp. Flour (60 ml.)
2 cups Milk, heated (500 ml.)
1/2 Tsp. Salt (2 ml.)
1/4 Tsp. Pepper (1 ml.)
1/2 Tsp. Dill Weed (2 ml.)
1 Cup Cheddar Cheese, grated (250 ml.)

Flake fish. Make a white sauce by cooking flour and fat together for 1 minute over a medium heat. Add milk, salt, pepper and dill. Bring to a boil and cook for 1 - 2 minutes or until mixture thickens. Remove from heat. Arrange flaked fish in a buttered baking dish. Cover with cream sauce and top with grated cheese. Bake in a 350°F (180°C) oven for 20 - 25 minutes. *Makes 6 servings.*
(Serve accompanied by vegetables or a green salad)

BAKED STUFFED COD

4 lb. Whole Fresh Cod (2 kg.)
2 Cups Fresh Bread Crumbs (500 ml.)
1 Medium Onion, finely chopped
1/2 Cup Chopped Celery (125 ml.)
1 Tsp. Thyme (5 ml.)
1/2 Tsp. Salt (2 ml.)
1 Tsp. Black Pepper (5 ml.)
1/4 Cup Melted Butter (50 ml.)

Clean fish, wash and sponge dry. in a bowl combine bread crumbs, onion, celery, thyme, salt and pepper. Add melted butter; mix well. Stuff fish with bread dressing. Fasten the opening with toothpicks or skewers. Place fish on a large buttered baking pan. Brush with additional melted butter. Bake in a 425°F (220°C) oven for approximately 25 - 30 minutes or until fish flakes with a fork.
Serves 6. (Boiled new potatoes and fresh peas accompany stuffed cod well)

CRAB CAKES

1 Cup Cooked Crab (250 ml.)
2 Tbsp. Butter (30 ml.)
2 Tbsp. Flour (30 ml.)
1 Cup Milk (250 ml.)
1 Clove Garlic, crushed
1/2 Tsp. Thyme (2 ml.)
2 Tbsp. Fresh Parsley, chopped (30 ml.)
1/2 Tsp. Salt (2 ml.)
1/4 Tsp. Pepper (1 ml.)
2 Cups Fresh Breadcrumbs (500 ml.)
1 Egg, beaten
6 Tbsp. Oil (90 ml.)

Cut crab meat in small pieces. Set aside. Melt butter in saucepan. Add flour, cook for 1 minute. Add milk, garlic, thyme, salt and pepper. Cook stirring constantly until sauce thickens (about 2 - 3 minutes). Fold in crab and parsley, mix well. Remove from heat and spread on large pan to cool quickly in refrigerator. Remove from refrigerator and divide into several portions. Shape into patties or cakes. Roll in fresh breadcrumbs. Dip in beaten egg and roll againin crumbs. Heat oil and fry cakes quickly for 5 minutes turning once. Drain on absorbent paper. Serve accompanied by tartar sauce. *Serves 6.*

FISH CAKES

1 lb. Salt Cod (500 g.)
4 Cups Mashed Potato (l L.)
1 Onion, finely chopped
2 Tbsp. Butter (30 ml.)
2 Eggs
1 Tsp. Thyme (5 ml.)
1/2 Tsp. Pepper (2 ml.)
1 Tsp. Salt (5 ml.)
1 Tbsp. Fresh Parsley, chopped (15 ml.)
Flour for Coating
Oil and Butter for Frying

Soak the salt cod overnight. Drain. Cover cod with cold water. Bring to a boil, reduce heat to simmer for 3 - 5 minutes. Drain and flake cod with a fork. Sauté the chopped onion in melted butter. Add to fish. Lightly beat the eggs with a fork. Add to fish mixture along with the mashed potato, thyme, salt, pepper and parsley. Combine mixture well and form into round cakes. Coat lightly with flour. Heat oil and butter in skillet. Fry cakes over medium heat for 2 - 3 minutes on each side until crisp and golden in colour.
Serves 6 - 8.

FISH AND BREWS

Our Newfoundland neighbours introduced this
delicacy to Cape Breton

1 1/2 lb. Salt Cod (750 g.)
4 Hard Bread Cakes
1/2 lb. Salt Pork, cubed (250 g.)

Soak salt cod in cold water overnight. (Cut in pieces if
necessary). Soak hard bread separately overnight.
(If cod is very salty, change water once during soaking
period). Drain fish and place in a saucepan and cover fish
with cold water. Bring to a boil and simmer uncovered for
10 - 15 minutes or until tender. Drain. In a skillet fry cubed
salt pork until golden. Drain the hard bread, place in a
saucepan. Cover with water and bring to a boil. Drain. Place
bread on plates, place fish on top and spoon on the
(scrunchions) cubed salt pork.
Serves 6.
*Note: In many Cape Breton homes blue potatoes are boiled and
served with the fish.*

OVEN BAKED MACKEREL

2 Mackerel
1 Large Onion, sliced
4 Tbsp. Butter, melted (60 ml.)
1 Tsp. Salt (5 ml.)
1/2 Tsp. Pepper (2 ml.)
1 Bay Leaf

Clean and wash the mackerel. Remove head, tail and fins.
Cut a slit along the back of the mackerel and slit it lengthwise.
Arrange the fish pieces in a casserole. Pour melted butter
over the fish. Season with salt and pepper. Lay onion rings
on top of the fish with bay leaf. Cover casserole dish tightly
with foil. Bake for 20 -25 minutes in a 375°F (180°C) oven.
Serves 4 -6.

Meats

CAPE BRETON BOILED DINNER

4 lbs. Corned Beef (2 kg.)
4 Qts. Cold Water (4 L.)
3 Large Onions
1 Large Turnip
4 Parsnip
4 Carrots
4 Potatoes
1 Head of Cabbage

Rinse the beef carefully. Prepare the vegetables and cut them in halves and quarters. Place the beef in a large pot and cover with cold water. Bring to a boil, drain. Cover the meat again with cold water and simmer for 3 hours or until tender. Carefully remove beef and place on a large platter and keep warm. Cook the vegetables in beef cooking water until tender. Drain vegetables and arrange around meat on platter.   *Serves 6 - 8*

CORNED BEEF HASH

2 Cups Cold Cooked Corned Beef (500 g.)
2 Cups Cooked Potatoes, diced (500 ml.)
1 Large Onion, chopped
1 Clove Garlic, minced
1/4 Cup Butter (60 ml.)
Salt and Pepper

Trim fat from corned beef and chop finely or grind. Cook potatoes and dice. Set aside. Melt butter in heavy skillet, add garlic, and onion and cook until soft. Combine corned beef, potatoes and onion mixture together. Season with salt and pepper. Place in buttered casserole and dot the top with butter. Bake in a 350°F (175°C) oven for 35 minutes. If desired, serve with poached eggs.
Variation: Corned beef hash can also be prepared using canned corned beef.
Serves 4.

LEFT: Main-A-Dieux   ABOVE: Highland Cattle, Middle River   OVERLEAF: Margaree

MINTED LAMB CHOPS

6 Lamb Chops
1/2 Cup Lemon Juice (125 ml.)
1/2 Cup White Wine (125 ml.)
4 Tbsp. Fresh Mint; chopped (60 ml.)
2 Cloves Garlic, crushed
1/2 Cup Honey (125 ml.)

Trim excess fat from the chops. Place chops in shallow pan.
Combine lemon juice, wine, mint, garlic and honey.
Pour over chops. Refrigerate for a few hours or overnight.
Place chops on prepared barbecue. Baste with marinade.
Cook until chops are tender. Serves 6.   Minted lamb can
also be prepared under the broiler. Have oven rack low to
allow time for basting.
Serves 6.

CAPE BRETON ROAST LEG OF LAMB

1 Leg of Lamb, 5 - 6 lbs. (2.5 - 3 kg.)
2 Large Garlic Cloves
Salt and Pepper to season
1 Tsp. Rosemary (5 ml.)
1 Cup Stock or Water
1 Onion, quartered
1 Carrot, sliced
4 Tbsp. Butter (60 ml.)

Place lamb on a rack in a roasting pan. Peel the garlic cloves
and cut into small slivers. Pierce the meat here and there
with small pointed knife and slide in a piece of garlic along
the knife blade of each incision. Season with salt, pepper and
rosemary. Arrange quartered onions and sliced carrot
around lamb. Place lamb in a 450°F (230°C) oven for 15
minutes. Reduce heat to 375°F (190°C) and pour stock or
water in roast pan. Roast lamb for an additional 15 - 20
minutes per pound. Baste meat several times while cooking.
Remove roast from oven and place on large platter and keep
warm. Whisk butter into juices in roaster. Bring to a boil.
Reduce to half, season with salt and pepper. Pour into sauce
boat and serve to accompany lamb.

VENISON STEW

4 lbs. Venison from Leg or Haunch (2 kg.)
4 Tbsp. Seasoned Flour (60 ml.)
4 Tbsp Olive Oil (60 ml.)
4 Medium Onions, coarsely chopped
4 Slices Bacon, chopped
Juice of l Lemon
1 Cup Port Wine (250 ml.)
2 Cups Beef Stock (500 ml.)
2 Cloves Garlic
1 Bay Leaf
1 Tsp. Pepper (5 ml.)
2 Tsp. Salt (10 ml.)

Cut trimmed venison in cubes and roll in seasoned flour. Heat oil in heavy skillet. Add the bacon and meat a few pieces at a time. Fry meat turning pieces as they brown. Remove meat to a heavy casserole. In remaining oil sauté onion and carrots. Arrange over venison. Add lemon juice, port, stock, garlic, bay leaf, salt and pepper. Cover and bring to a boil. Reduce and simmer for l l/2 - 2 hours or until venison is tender. *Serve with boiled potatoes. Carrots and turnip can be added to stew if desired.*

VENISON POT ROAST

4 lbs. Rump Shoulder Neck (2 Kg.)
4 Large Onions, sliced
2 Cloves Garlic
1 Bay Leaf
1 Tsp. Pepper (5 ml.)
2 Tsp. Salt (10 ml.)
1 Tsp. Thyme (5 ml.)
3 Tbsp. Oil (45ml.)
1 Cup Seasoned Flour (250 ml.)
2 Cups Stock or Water (500 ml.)

Roll meat in seasoned flour. Heat oil in heavy cooking pot and brown meat on all sides. Add onions, garlic, bay leaf, salt, pepper, thyme and stock or water. Cover, bring to a boil. Reduce and simmer over low heat until meat is tender 2 1/2 - 3 hours. One half hour before meat is done add a selection of vegetables such as carrots, turnip, parsnip and potatoes. Remove meat to large heated platter. Arrange vegetables around meat. Keep warm. With stock make a rich gravy. Combine 3 tbsp (45 ml.) cornstarch with 4 tbsp cold water (60 ml.). bring stock to a boil. Add cornstarch and cook until thickened. Serve with venison. *Serves 6.*

Desserts & Preserves

STRAWBERRY SHORTCAKE

In Cape Breton strawberry festivals abound. The shortcake is most commonly made with a rich, sweet tea biscuit dough.

2 Cups Flour (500 ml.)
4 Tsp. Baking Powder (20 ml.)
1 Tsp. Salt (5 ml.)
2 Tbsp. Sugar (30 ml.)
1/2 Cup Butter (125 ml.)
1/4 Cup Shortening 50 ml.)
1 Egg
3/4 Cup Milk (175 ml.)

Measure flour in mixing bowl. Add baking powder, salt and sugar. work in butter and shortening with pastry blender until mixture resembles coarse meal. Whisk egg with milk. Reserve two tablespoons of mixture. Add to remaining ingredients all at once and stir with a fork until moistened. Knead lightly on a floured surface 10 times. Cut in desired sizes and place on a baking sheet. Brush tops with reserved egg mixture. Bake in a 425°F (220°C) for 8 - 10 minutes. Cool. Split and top with sweetened strawberries and garnish with whipped cream.
Serves 6 - 8.

DUNDEE CAKE

1 Cup Butter (250 ml.)
1 Cup Sugar (250 ml.)
5 Eggs
2 1/2 Cups Flour (625 ml.)
1 Tsp. Baking Powder (5 ml.)
1/2 Tsp. Salt (2 ml.)
1 Cup Sultana Raisins (250 ml.)
1 Cup Currants (250 ml.)
1 Cup sliced Almonds (250 ml.)
1 Cup Mixed Candied Fruit (250 ml.)
1 Tbsp. Orange Rind, grated (15 ml.)
1 Tbsp. Lemon Rind, grated (15 ml.)
2 Tbsp. Orange Juice (30 ml.)
Almond halves and candied cherries to decorate

Cream butter and sugar until light. Beat in eggs one at a time, beating after each addition. Combine flour, baking powder and salt. Mix in raisins, currants, almonds, candied fruit, orange and lemon rind. Add to creamed mixture with orange juice. Mix well. Grease and line a 9 inch (22 cm.) tube pan with brown paper. Grease paper. Spoon batter in pan. Spread evenly. Decorate top with almonds and cherries. Bake in a 300°F (150°C) oven approximately 1 hour and 15 minutes, or until tester comes out clean. Cool, remove from pan. Wrap tightly in foil and allow to mellow for several days before serving.

MAPLE SYRUP CAKE

2 1/2 Cups Flour (625 ml.)
3 Tsp. Baking Powder (15 ml.)
1 Tsp. Baking Soda (5 ml.)
1 Tsp. Salt (5 ml.)
1/2 Cup Butter (125 ml.)
1/2 Cup Brown Sugar (125 ml.)
1 Tsp. Vanilla(5 ml.)
2 Eggs
1 Cup Maple Syrup (250 ml.)
1/2 Cup Hot Water (125 ml.)

Measure flour. Combine with baking powder, soda and salt. Cream butter, sugar and vanilla until light. Add eggs one at a time beating well after each addition. Add dry ingredients to creamed mixture alternately with combined syrup and hot water starting and ending with dry ingredients. Mix well after each addition. Do not over beat. Divide batter evenly between two greased and floured 8" (20 x 5 cm.) round layer cake pans. Bake 375°F (190°C) for 25 - 30 minutes or until tester inserted in center comes out clean. Turn out to cool on cooling rack. Frost with maple syrup frosting.

MAPLE SYRUP FROSTING

1/2 Cup Maple Syrup (125 ml.)
1 Cup Brown Sugar, lightly packed (250 ml.)
1 Egg White
1 Tsp. Vanilla (5 ml.)
Pinch of Salt

Combine all ingredients in top of double boiler. Place over boiling water and beat constantly with electric mixer at high speed. Beat until frosting stands in stiff peaks, about 6 - 7 minutes. Remove from heat. Sufficient to frost an 8" (20 x 5 cm.) layer cake.

SHORTBREAD

1 Cup Soft Butter (250 ml.)
1/2 Cup Brown Sugar (125 ml.)
2 Cups Flour (500 ml.)
1 Tsp. Vanilla (5 ml.)

In a bowl, cream butter and sugar until light and creamy. Gradually add the flour 1/4 cup (50 ml.) at a time mixing well after each addition. Add just enough so dough can be gathered into a ball. Knead dough on a floured surface until smooth. Roll dough to 1/4" thickness. Cut in desired shapes with floured cutter. Place on ungreased baking sheet. Bake 300F (150°C) for 15 - 20 minutes or until lightly browned.

Variations: To make petticoat tarts, divide shortbread in two pieces. Pat dough into a round 9 inch (22 x 5 cm.) cake pan. Prick all over with fork. Bake as directed and score into wedges.

RICH SCONES

2 Cups Flour (500 ml.)
4 Tsp. Baking Powder (20 ml.)
1/4 Cup Sugar (50 ml.)
1 Tsp. Salt (5 ml.)
1/2 Cup Butter or Shortening (125 ml.)
1/2 Cup Currants (125 ml.)
1/2 Cup Milk (125 ml.)
2 Eggs

Measure flour in a bowl. Add baking powder, sugar and salt. Work butter or shortening into flour mixture until it resembles coarse meal. Add currants. Combine eggs and milk. Stir into flour mixture and mix until well moistened. Turn out on a lightly floured surface and knead 20 times. Shape dough into a circle 1/2" (1.25 cm.) thick. Brush with milk and sprinkle with sugar. Cut into 12 pie-shaped wedges and place on greased baking sheet. Bake 425°F (220°C) oven for 12 - 15 minutes. Serve hot with butter and preserves.
Makes 1 dozen scones.
Note: Raisins can be substituted for currants.

RAISIN PIE

2 Cups Raisins (500 ml.)
2 Cups Cold Water (500 ml.)
3/4 Cup Brown Sugar (175 ml.)
2 Tbsp. Flour (30 ml.)
2 Tbsp. Lemon Juice (30 ml.)
2 Tsp. Lemon Rind (10 ml.)
1 Tsp. Vanilla (5 ml.)
1 Tbsp. Butter (15 ml.)

In a saucepan combine raisins and water. Heat to boiling. Cover and simmer for 10 minutes. Mix together brown sugar and flour. Stir into raisin mixture. Cook over medium heat stirring constantly until mixture comes to a boil, thickens and has a shiny colour. Remove from heat, add lemon juice, rind, vanilla and butter. Mix and cool. Pour filling into pastry lined 9 inch (23 cm.) tart shell. Cover with either lattice top or full top crust, flute edges. Make slits for steam to escape. Bake in a 400°F (200°C) oven for 25 minutes or until crust is brown.

Cabot Trail.

PORK PIES

A unique Cape Breton sweet that is traditional at family gatherings.

BASE:
>1 Cup Butter (250 ml.)
>1/2 Cup Brown Sugar (125 ml.)
>1 Tsp. Vanilla (5 ml.)
>2 Cups Flour (500 ml.)

DATE FILLING:

>2 Cups Dates, cut up (500 ml.)
>1 Cup Brown Sugar (250 ml.)
>1 Cup Water (250 ml.)
>1 Tbsp. Lemon Juice (15 ml.)
>1 Tsp. Lemon Rind (5 ml.)
>1 Tsp. Vanilla (5ml.)
>2 Tbsp. Butter (30 ml.)

Cream butter, sugar and vanilla until light and fluffy. Gradually add the flour combining well to form a dough. Press small amounts of dough in mini-sized tart tins. Bake in a 350°F (180°C) oven for 10 - 12 minutes. Remove from tins. Cool and top with date filling. To make date filling, combine dates, sugar, water, lemon juice and rind in a saucepan. Cook over medium heat until dates are soft, stirring frequently. Remove from heat, add the butter and vanilla. Fill the tart shells with a small amount of date filling. Ice with butter icing. *Makes 3 dozen pork pies.*

BUTTER ICING

>2 Cups Icing Sugar (500 ml.)
>1/4 Cup Butter (50 ml.)
>3 Tbsp. Milk (45 ml.)
>1/2 Tsp. Maple Flavouring (2 ml.)

Combine icing sugar, butter, milk and flavouring in mixing bowl. Beat until light and fluffy. Make rosettes in the center of each Pork Pie.

BANNOCK

>3 Cups Flour (750 ml.)
>1 Tbsp. White Sugar (15 ml.)
>6 Tsp. Baking Powder (30 ml.)
>1 Tsp. Salt (5 ml.)
>3 Tbsp. Shortening (45 ml.)
>1 Cup Milk (250 ml.)

In a bowl combine the flour, sugar, baking powder and salt. Work in shortening until it is a mealy texture. Pour in the milk all at once and mix just enough to combine. Pour batter into a greased 9 x 9 inch (22 x 22 cm.) pan. Bake in a 400°F (200°C) oven 25 - 30 minutes. *Serve with butter and jam. Variations: Substitute 1 cup (250 g.) of whole wheat flour for 1 Cup of white flour; or 1/2 Cup (125 ml.) of rolled oats for 1/2 cup (125 ml.) of flour. Add raisins, currants or cranberries to the batter.*

TEA BISCUITS

>2 cups Flour (500 ml.)
>4 Tsp. Baking Powder (20 ml.)
>1 Tsp. Salt (5 ml.)
>3/4 cup Milk
>1/2 Cup Shortening (125 ml.)
>1 Egg

Measure flour and pour into mixing bowl. Add baking powder and salt. Cut in shortening with pastry blender until mixture resembles coarse meal. Add milk all at once and stir with a fork until all ingredients are moistened. Turn onto a floured surface and knead lightly 10 times. Roll out dough to 1/2 inch (1 cm.) in thickness. Cut with 2 inch (5 cm.) cutter. Place 1 inch (2 cm.) apart on baking sheet. Whisk egg with a fork. Brush tops of biscuits with egg mixture. Bake 425°F (220°C) for 8 - 10 minutes. *Makes 1 dozen biscuits.*

GINGER BREAD

>2 Cups Flour (500 ml.)
>2 Tsp. Baking Powder (10 ml.)
>1 Tsp. Soda (5 ml.)
>1/2 Tsp. Salt (2 ml.)
>2 Tsp. Cinnamon (10 ml.)
>2 Tsp. Ginger (10 ml.)
>1/2 Tsp. Cloves (2 ml.)
>1/2 Cup Shortening (125 ml.)
>1/2 Cup Sugar (125ml.)
>2 Eggs
>1 Cup Molasses (250 ml.)
>1 Cup Boiling Water (250 ml.)

Combine flour, baking powder, soda, salt, cinnamon, ginger and cloves. Cream shortening, sugar and eggs thoroughly. Add molasses to mixture. Stir in boiling water. Mix well. Pour batter in a greased and floured 9 inch (22 x 22 cm) square pan. Bake 350°F (180°C) for 40 - 45 minutes or until tester inserted in center comes out clean.
Serve warm with sweetened whipped cream or lemon sauce.

MOLASSES COOKIES

>1 Cup Molasses (250 ml.)
>1 Tbsp. Soda (15ml.)
>1 Tbsp. Vinegar (15 ml.)
>1 Cup Lard (250 ml.)
>1 Cup Brown Sugar (250 ml.)
>1 Egg
>2 Tsp. Ground Ginger (10 ml.)
>1 Tsp. Salt (5 ml.)
>4 Cups Flour (1 L.)

In a heavy saucepan, bring molasses and lard to a boil. Add soda and vinegar. Combine well and cool. To cooled mixture add egg, brown sugar and dry ingredients. Mix well and chill for 1 hour. Roll dough thin. Cut in 2 inch (5 cm.) circles. Place on lightly greased cookie sheet. Bake in a 350°F (180°C) oven for 8 - 10 minutes or until crisp. *Makes 4 - 5 doz.*

POTATO SCONES

2 Cups Flour (500 ml.)
1/2 Cup Granulated Sugar (125 ml.)
4 Tsp. Baking Powder (20 ml.)
1 Tsp. Salt (5 ml.)
1/3 Cup Shortening or Butter (75 ml.)
1/2 Cup Raisins or Currants (125 ml.)
1 Cup Potatoes, mashed (250 ml.)
1 Cup Milk (250 ml.)
2 Eggs
1 Tbsp. Milk (15 ml.)

Combine flour, sugar, baking powder, salt and sugar in a bowl. Cut in shortening or butter until mixture resembles coarse meal. Stir in raisins. Whisk eggs lightly with a fork and add milk. Combine mashed potatoes with dry ingredients using a fork. Stir milk mixture into dry ingredients to moisten. Kneed on floured surface for 4 - 5 minutes. Pat into a circle 1/2 inch (l cm.) thick. Place on ungreased baking sheet. Brush with milk. Sprinkle with sugar. Cut in 16 wedges allowing a small space between each wedge. Bake 425°F (220°C) oven for approx. 12 - 15 minutes.
Note: Can be served with scrambled eggs.

FAT ARCHIES

1 Cup Shortening (250 ml.)
1 Cup Sugar (250 ml.)
1 Cup Molasses (250 ml.)
2 Eggs
3 Tsp. Baking Soda (15 ml.)
3/4 Cup Boiling Water 175 ml.)
4 Cups Flour(1 L.)
1 Tsp. Cinnamon (5 ml.)
1 Tsp. Cloves (5 ml.)
1 Tsp. Ginger (5 ml.)
1 Tsp. Cream of Tartar (5 ml.)
1 Tsp. Salt (5 ml.)

Cream together shortening and sugar until light. Add molasses and eggs and beat well. Dissolve soda in boiling water and add to creamed mixture. Combine flour with cinnamon, cloves, ginger, cream of tartar and salt. Add gradually to molasses mixture, mixing well after each addition. Dough should be firm; chill. Roll on floured surface to 1/4 inch thickness. Place on greased baking sheet and bake 375°F (190°C) oven for 8 - 10 minutes.
Makes 4 - 5 dozen.

Inverness Beach.

UPSIDE DOWN APPLE PIE

4 Tbsp. Soft Butter (60 ml.)
1/2 Cup Brown Sugar (125 ml.)
1/2 Cup Pecan Halves (125 ml.)
6 Cups Apples, peeled and sliced (1.2 L.)
1 Cup Granulated Sugar (250 ml.)
1 1/2 Tsp. Cinnamon (7 ml.)

PASTRY:

2 Cups Flour (500 ml.)
1 Tsp. Salt (5 ml.)
1/2 Cup Shortening (125 ml.)
1/4 Cup Butter (50 ml.)
5 - 6 Tbsp. Cold Water (70 - 90 ml.)

This pie is made in a heavy bottomed steel fry pan. Melt butter in skillet. Add brown sugar and combine over low heat until sugar caramelizes. Arrange pecan halves in caramelized sugar. Combine apple slices, sugar and cinnamon. Spread evenly over pecans. Place skillet on low heat and allow apples to start cooking mixing apples carefully from time to time. To prepare pastry, mix flour and salt in a bowl. Work in shortening and butter until mixture is like coarse meal. Add water. Mix with a fork and form into a ball (chill if time allows). Roll out pastry in a circle the size of the skillet. Place pastry over apples tucking pastry down the sides of skillet. Make two slashes in center of pastry to allow steam to escape. Place in a preheated 400°F (200°C) oven for 35 - 40 minutes or until apples are tender and pastry is golden. Invert on a serving plate. Arrange apples and pecans if necessary. *Serve warm. Makes 10 inch pie.*

RHUBARB STRAWBERRY PRESERVES

4 Cups Rhubarb, cut up (1 L.)
4 Cups Strawberries, sliced (1 L.)
3 Cups Granulated Sugar (750 ml.)
1 Tbsp. Lemon Juice

Wash rhubarb and cut in 1/2 inch pieces. Wash berries, hull and slice. Place in a large pot and add lemon juice. Cook over a medium heat, stirring fruit for 20 minutes to extract juices. Add sugar, bring to a boil stirring until sugar is dissolved. Reduce heat and simmer mixture until thick and clear, approximately 25 minutes. Remove from heat, stir for five minutes. Ladle into sterilized jars and seal.

STRAWBERRY JAM

8 Cups Prepared Strawberries (2 L.)
8 Cups Sugar (2 L.)
1/2 Cup Lemon Juice (125 ml.)

Wash, hull and slice sufficient berries to measure the amount required, about 2 1 Quart, (1 L) boxes. Place berries in preserving pot, add sugar and lemon juice. Combine well. Place over high heat and bring to a boil uncovered for 15 - 20 minutes or until mixture reaches the jam stage and is thick. Remove from heat, stir for 5 minutes. Ladle into hot sterilized jars and seal. *Approximately 8 - 6 oz. jars.*

BLUEBERRY JAM

4 Cups Blueberries (1 L.)
3 Tbsp. Lemon Juice (45 ml.)
4 Cups Granulated Sugar (1 L.)

Combine cleaned blueberries and lemon juice in a large saucepan. Bring to a boil. Simmer covered for about 20 minutes or until blueberries are soft. Stir in sugar, stirring continuously until sugar is dissolved. Bring to a boil uncovered for about 20 minutes or until jam jells when tested. Remove from heat and stir for 5 minutes to avoid floating fruit. Pour into hot sterilized jars and seal. *Makes 4 cups.*

RASPBERRY JAM

4 Cups Raspberries (1 L.)
1 Tbsp. Lemon Juice (30 ml.)
4 Cups Granulated Sugar (1 kg.)

Combine raspberries and lemon juice in large saucepan. Cook over medium heat for 10 minutes until raspberries are soft. Stir in sugar over heat stirring continuously until sugar is dissolved. Bring to a boil. Boil uncovered for 10 - 15 minutes or until jam jells when tested. Stir for 5 minutes to avoid floating fruit. Pour into hot sterilized jars and seal. *Makes 4 cups.*

PEACH JAM

12 Cups Prepared Peaches (3 L.)
6 Cups Sugar (1.2 L.)
4 Tbsp. Lemon Juice (60 ml.)

Wash peaches and blanch in boiling water for 30 - 60 seconds depending on ripeness of fruit. Plunge in cold water. Remove skins, pit and cut in pieces. Measure the prepared fruit and place in a large preserving pot. Add sugar and lemon juice. Combine well and allow to stand for 1 hour. Place over high heat. Bring to a boil. Boil uncovered until mixture thickens and reaches jam stage about 20 - 25 minutes stirring occasionally. Remove from heat. Stir for 5 minutes and ladle into hot sterilized jars and seal. *Makes approximately 12 - 6 oz. jars.*

PUMPKIN PRESERVES

8 Cups Pumpkin, cubed (2 L.)
4 Cups Granulated Sugar (1 L.)
2 Lemons, rind and juice
1 Tbsp. Grated Fresh Ginger (15 ml.)

Peel, clean and remove seeds of pumpkin. Cut pumpkin in cubes and layer with sugar in large bowl. Cover and let stand overnight at room temperature. Stir mixture twice and place in a large saucepan. Add lemon rind, juice and grated fresh ginger. Boil for 40 - 50 minutes or until pumpkin is tender and transparent. Remove from heat. Stir for 5 minutes. Pour into hot, sterilized jars and seal. *Approx. 4 cups.*

POLISH

Collected by MR. MIKE PIERRYNOWSKI

OLD FASHIONED POLISH DILL PICKLES

1 Gallon Pickling Cukes (4 L.)
2 1/2 Quarts Water (2.5 L.)
1/2 Cup Coarse Salt (125 ml.)
1/4 Cup Vinegar (50 ml.)
2 - 3 Cloves Garlic, peeled
Fresh Dill, several sprigs

Wash pickling cucumbers and place in a sterilized gallon jar or crock. Combine water, salt and vinegar in saucepan and bring to a boil. Boil 5 minutes and cool. Pour mixture over cukes. Insert sprigs of fresh dill and garlic cloves. Cucumbers must be submerged in the brine (weigh them down if necessary). *Pickles will be ready in approximately six (6) weeks.*

KAPUSTA

1 Cup Lima Beans (250 ml.)
8 Cups Sauerkraut (2 L.)
2 Onions, diced
4 Pork Chops
1 Cup Mushrooms, sliced (250 ml.)
1 Bay Leaf
Salt and Pepper as needed

Cook the lima beans in salted water until tender. In a large skillet, cook the pork chops. Turn chops twice during cooking. Remove chops and set aside. Using pan drippings and 3 tbsp. (45 ml.) flour and 3 cups (750 ml.) of stock or water, make a rich brown gravy. Return chops to gravy and simmer chops in gravy for 10 minutes. To chops and gravy, add drained lima beans, onion, sauerkraut, mushrooms, bay leaf, salt and pepper. Cover and simmer gently for 30 minutes or until sauerkraut is tender.
Serve with mashed potatoes and vegetables.   Serves 4.

POTATO SALAD WITH LEMON & OIL

3 Large Potatoes, boiled, peeled
3 -4 Green Onion Tops, chopped
1/4 Cup Oil (50 ml)
1/4 Cup Fresh Lemon Juice (50 ml)
1/2 Tsp. Salt (2ml)
1/4 Tsp. Pepper (1ml)

Cook potatoes, whole with skins, in boiling water until tender. Cool, peel and dice into a bowl. Chop green onion and add to potatoes. Season with salt and pepper. Mix lemon juice and oil together and pour over potatoes. Mix to combine. Place in the refrigerator until ready to serve. Will keep for several days. *Serves 4 -6.*

RIGHT: St. Mary's Polish Church, Sydney

BORSCHT (*Beet Soup*)

2 Qts Beef Stock (2 L)
2 Cups Red Beets, shredded (500 ml)
1 Onion Diced
1 Stalk Celery
1 Large Carrot, diced
1 Tbsp. Vinegar or Lemon Juice (15ml)
Salt
Pepper
1 Cup Sour Cream (250 ml)

Place vegetables in a large saucepan, cover with beef stock. Add vinegar. Cook for approximately one hour, until vegetables are tender. Add salt and pepper to taste. Place sour cream in a small bowl. Slowly add 1 cup (250 ml) of hot soup, a few tablespoons at a time to sour cream until mixture is smooth. Return to soup. Stir well and serve.
Serves 6 - 8

PEROGIES

BASIC DOUGH:

4 Cups Flour (1 L.)
2 Eggs
1/4 Cup Oil (50 ml.)
1 1/4 Cups Milk or Water (300 ml.)
1/2 Tsp. Salt (2 ml.)

Combine all ingredients and mix. Form into a ball. Cover and let rest for 30 minutes. Roll dough to about 1/8 inch thickness. Cut the dough into circles, about 3 inches (7 cm.) in diameter with a cookie cutter dipped in flour. Place approximately a tablespoon of filling in the center of each circle. Bring edges of dough together to form a half circle. Press edges together. Place filled perogies on baking sheet. Cover with a cloth until ready for boiling. Fill a large pot 3/4 full of water. Bring to boil. Add 2 tbsp. salt and l tbsp. oil. With water boiling, cook about 12 perogies at a time. Boil about 5 minutes or until perogies rise to the top of the water. Remove from water with a slotted spoon and arrange on a tray. Pour a little melted butter over the perogies to keep them from sticking. Serve with sautéed onions and a spoon of sour cream.

POTATO-CHEESE FILLING

6 Large Potatoes, boiled and mashed
1/2 lb. of Old Cheddar Cheese, grated (250 g.)
2 Tbsp. Butter (30 ml.)
Pepper to taste

SAUERKRAUT-MUSHROOM FILLING

4 Cups Sauerkraut, cooked (1 L)
1 Large Onion, chopped
4 Tbsp. Oil (60 ml)
1 Cup Mushrooms, minced (250 ml)
1 Tsp. Caraway Seed (5 ml)
Salt and pepper to taste

Combine ingredients above and mix well.
Cool and use as filling in perogies.

UKRAINIAN

Collected by MRS. WANDA HUK

POTATO PANCAKES

1 lb. Potatoes (500 g.)
3/4 Cup Flour (175 ml.)
1 Egg, beaten
1 Tsp. Baking Powder (5 ml.)
1 Tsp. Salt (5 ml.)
1/2 Onion, grated

Grate potatoes, add egg and onion. Add dry ingredients gradually, mix well. Drop 1 Tbsp. of batter at a time on a hot greased skillet and brown on both sides.
Serve hot with heavy sour cream.
Serves 4

HOLUBTSI (Cabbage Rolls)

BUCKWHEAT FILLING:

1 Large Head of Cabbage (1)
1 Large Onion, chopped (1)
1/4 Cup Oil (50 ml.)
2 Cups Buckwheat, dried in oven (500 ml.)
1 Tbsp. Salt (15 ml.)
5 Cups Boiling Water (1 L.)
4 Tbsp. Margarine (60 ml.)
2 - 3 Medium Boiled Potatoes, mashed
1 Cup Water (250 ml.)
2 Tbsp. Oil (30 ml.)
1/2 Tsp. Salt (2 ml.)

To dry buckwheat, spread on a baking pan and place in 200°F (100°C) oven for 15 minutes. Mix buckwheat with margarine. Add salt and boiling water. Bring to a boil. Cover and simmer 25 minutes. Sauté onions in oil and mix with mashed potatoes and buckwheat. Set aside to cool. Remove core from cabbage. Place cabbage in large pot of boiling water. Add salt and cook until leaves are soft. Separate leaves. Line a casserole dish with a few leaves. Place a heaping spoonful of filling on each remaining leaf. Fold sides over and roll up. Place in layers in casserole. Combine water, oil and salt. Pour over Holubtsi. Cover and bake 350°F oven for 1 1/2 - 2 hours.
Serves 6.

PASKA (Easter Bread)

1/2 Cup Lukewarm Water (125 ml.)
1 Tsp. Granulated Sugar (5 ml.)
1 Tbsp. Yeast (15 ml.)
6 Eggs, beaten (6)
1/4 Cup Granulated Sugar (50 ml.)
1/4 Cup Melted Butter (50 ml.)
1 Tbsp. Salt (15 ml.)
3 Cups Lukewarm Water (750 ml.)
9 Cups Flour (2.2 L.)
1 Egg, beaten for glazing

Combine lukewarm water, yeast and sugar in a small bowl. Allow to sit for 3 - 4 minutes until foamy. In a large bowl combine beaten eggs, sugar, melted butter, salt and lukewarm water. Mix in 8 Cups (2L.) of flour. Sprinkle remaining flour on table and knead dough until smooth and elastic (dough must be fairly stiff). Cover and let rise in a warm place until double. Punch down and let rise again. Butter 2 - 9 inch (22 x 5 cm.) round bake pans. Punch down dough a second time and divide into 3 equal pieces. Divide one piece in two to cover pans. Flatten pieces to fit into bottom of prepared pan approximately 1" thick. Roll each of the remaining pieces of dough in your hand to 36 inches (90 cm.) ropes length. Lay ropes of dough side by side on work table. Starting from the centre, braid the length repeating for other half of braid. Cut braid in two. Place braid in a circle along edge of each prepared base, continuing in a circle to completely cover the base. Cover with cloth. Let rise until double in size. Brush with beaten egg. Bake in a 400°F (200°C) oven for 15 minutes. Lower heat to 350°F (180°C) and bake for an additional 40 minutes.
Makes 2 Loaves

HOLIDAY HONEY CAKE

1 Cup Honey (250 ml.)
1 Cup Brown Sugar (250 ml.)
6 Egg Yolks
6 Egg Whites
1 Cup Soft, Unsalted Butter (250 g.)
3 1/2 Cups Flour (875 ml.)
1 Tsp. Baking Soda (5 ml.)
1 Tsp. Baking Powder (5 ml.)
1/2 Tsp. Cloves (2 ml.)
1 Tsp. Cinnamon (5 ml.)
1 Cup Walnuts, finely chopped (250 ml.)

Bring the honey and brown sugar to a boil. Remove from heat. Cool for 5 minutes and add egg yolks, one at a time, and beat well after each addition. Add the soft butter and beat until mixture is thick and creamy. Measure the dry ingredients and fold into creamed mixture. Add the walnuts and combine well. Beat the egg whites until soft peaks form and fold into the batter. Pour batter into a well-greased and paper lined 10 x 4 1/2inch (4 L.) tube pan or two 9 X 5 X 2 1/2 inch (2 L.) pans. Bake in a 350°F (180°C) oven for 1 hour. Remove from oven, allow to sit for 5 minutes and turn out on wire rack to cool.

RIGHT: Holy Ghost Ukrainian Church, Sydney

POPPY SEED CAKE

1/2 Cup Poppy Seed (125 ml.)
1 Cup Milk (250 ml.)
1 Tsp. Vanilla (5 ml.)
3/4 Cup Shortening (175 ml.)
1 1/2 Cups Sugar (375 ml.)
2 Cups Cake Flour (500 ml.)
2 Tsp. Baking Powder (10 ml.)
1/2 Tsp. Salt (2 ml.)
4 Egg Whites (4)

Soak poppy seed in milk. Add vanilla. Cream shortening.
Add sugar and beat well. Stir in sifted flour with soaked
poppy seeds. Beat egg whites stiffly and fold into mixture.
Grease and dust with flour, 2, layer cake pans. Divide batter
between two 8 inch (20 x 5 cm.) pans. Bake 350°F (180°C)
oven for 30 minutes. Frost with 7 minute frosting. This looks
like a polka dot cake with the white batter and little black
specks of poppy seed. Serves 6 - 8.

AFRO-CARRIBEAN

Collected by MRS. CLOTILDA YAKIMCHUK

CHICKEN PELAU

1 Chicken, cut in pieces, skin removed
1 Tin Cooked Red Kidney Beans (500 ml.)
2 Cups Long Grain Rice (500 ml.)
1 Onion, chopped
2 Cloves Garlic
1 Tbsp. Thyme, chopped (15 ml.) or
l Tsp. Thyme, dried (5 ml.)
2 Ripe Tomatoes, chopped
1 Tsp. Hot Pepper Sauce (5 ml.)
1 Tsp. Salt (5 ml.)
1 Tbsp. Oil (15 ml.)
1 Tbsp. Sugar (15 ml.)
3 Cups Chicken Stock or Water (750 ml.)

Wash and dry chicken pieces. Season with salt, pepper, onion and thyme. Allow to sit for awhile at room temperature or overnight in the fridge. Heat oil in a large heavy pot. Add sugar and continue heating until sugar turns deep brown. Add chicken pieces all at once and stir vigorously until each piece is coated with oil and sugar mixture. Reduce heat and continue stirring. Add the tomatoes, garlic, hot pepper sauce to chicken and stir well. Cover and cook over med. to low heat for about 30 - 40 mins. Add some water if necessary. Add kidney beans and liquid - bring to a boil. Add rice with water or stock. Mix well. Cover tightly and allow to continue cooking for an additional 20 - 25 mins. or until water is absorbed and rice is cooked.

JERK CHICKEN

6 Chicken Breasts or Quarters, skin removed
1 Large Onion, chopped
1 Lime, freshly squeezed
1/2 Cup Orange Juice (125 ml.)
3/4 Cup Vinegar (175 ml.)
1/4 Cup Soya Sauce (50 ml.)
1/4 Cup Oil (50 ml.)
1 Tbsp. Ground Allspice (15 ml.)
1 Tbsp. Dried Thyme (15 ml.)
2 Tbsp. Ground Sage (30 ml.)
1 Tbsp. Black Pepper (15 ml.)
1 Tsp. Cinnamon (5 ml.)
2 Tsp. Salt (10 ml.)
2 Tbsp. Crushed Garlic (30 ml.)
1 Tbsp. Sugar (15 ml.)

Mix all ingredients except chicken. Add chicken, stir to coat well. Cover and marinate 6 hrs or overnight in refrigerator. Grill over med. heat 6 min. on each side until cooked. Baste frequently with marinade. Bring remaining marinade to a boil. Simmer until reduced to a thick sauce. *Serve with rice.*

FISH SOUP

3 - 4 lb. Haddock, whole if possible (1.5 Kg. - 2 Kg.)
1 Onion, chopped
2 Cloves Garlic, chopped
1 Tsp. Salt (5 ml.)
1/2 Tsp. Black Pepper (2 ml.)
1 Whole Hot Green Pepper
1/2 Tsp. Thyme (2 ml.)
5 - 6 leaves Spanish Thyme, finely chopped
1 Lime, freshly squeezed
2 Tsp. Soya Sauce (10 ml.)
1 Tbsp. Butter or Margarine (15 ml.)
1 lb. Potatoes (500 g.)
1 1/2 lb. Assorted Root Vegetables, any combination of cassava,
dasheen, eddoes, yam, sweet potatoes (750 g.)
3 - 4 Green Bananas
6 Okras
1 Cup Elbow Macaroni

Scale fish and wash thoroughly. Cut into 1 inch thick steaks. Sprinkle salt, onions, garlic, thyme, black pepper and lime juice over fish and rub in. Marinate for 2 - 3 hours. Peel root vegetables, potatoes and green bananas. Wash, and cut into thick chunks. Put vegetables in a large pot, cover with water and bring to a boil. Parboil for 10 - 15 minutes making sure they are only slightly cooked. Layer okras and macaroni on vegetables. Add more water to just cover and continue simmering for another 10 minutes. Place fish slices on top of vegetables, add marinade and butter. Place green pepper in centre. Cover and simmer until cooked. With slotted spoon, remove pepper and fish slices. Discard pepper. Ladle vegetables and broth into soup bowls. Top with slice of fish.

LEFT & ABOVE: St. Phillips African Orthodox Church, Sydney

HOT MILK SPONGE CAKE

1 Cup Sifted All-Purpose Flour (250 ml.)
1 Tsp. Baking Powder (5 ml.)
1/4 Tsp. Salt (1 ml.)
1/2 Cup Milk (125 ml.)
2 Tbsp. Butter (30 ml.)
2 Eggs
1 Cup Sugar (250 ml.)
1 Tsp. Vanilla (5 ml.)

Preheat oven to 350°F (180°C). Sift together flour, salt, baking powder. Heat milk and butter until butter melts; keep hot. Using high speed on electric mixer, beat eggs until thick and lemon coloured (about 3 minutes). Using medium speed, gradually add in sugar. Beat about 4 - 5 minutes. Stir flour mixture into egg mixture until well blended, then stir in hot milk mixture and vanilla; blend well. Pour batter into well-greased and floured square pan (8 X 8 ", 20 X 20 cm.). Bake at 350°F (180°C) for 30 minutes. Cool in pan, DO NOT invert.

HOLIDAY TRIFLE

4 1/2 oz. Vanilla Custard Pudding (140 g.)
2 Cups Evaporated Milk (500 ml.)
2 Tbsp. Light Rum, optional (30 ml.)
2 1/2 Cups Whipping Cream (625 ml.)
3 Tbsp. Granulated Sugar (45 ml.)
4 Tbsp. Raspberry Jam (60 ml.)
1 - 8 inch Square Sponge Cake (20 cm.)
1/2 Cup Brandy and Sherry (125 ml.) (50 ml. each)
2 Cups Whole Strawberries or Bananas
Brandy or Sherry as needed

Blend custard and evaporated milk in saucepan. Cook, stirring occasionally, over medium heat, until mixture boils and thickens. Remove saucepan from heat and add rum; chill. Beat 1 cup of whipping cream and 1 tbsp. sugar until stiff. Fold into chilled pudding. Coat a deep glass bowl with raspberry jam. Cut cake into cubes. Put 1/3 of the cubes into the glass bowl. Sprinkle cake with brandy or sherry. Top with 1/3 of the custard, repeat procedure utilizing the remaining cake and custard. Beat remaining cream and garnish top of trifle.   *Serves 6 - 8.*

ABOVE: Carribean Sampler, Executive Chef Russell Weir, Sydney Delta Hotel.

JEWISH

Collected by MRS. EDITH LECKER

CHICKEN SOUP

6 lbs. Cut up Chicken Pieces (3 kgs.)
Cold Water, as needed
4 Ice Cubes
1 Carrot, peeled and cut in quarters
1 Onion, peeled and cut in quarters
4 Sprigs Parsley
1 Tsp. Salt (15 ml.)
White Pepper, freshly ground as needed

Rinse chicken pieces and remove excessive fat. Arrange pieces in cooking pot. Add water. Do not completely cover chicken. Bring to a boil over high heat. Add ice cubes and immediately lower the heat (to stop soup from boiling rapidly). Skim the froth from the soup very slowly so it will be clear, not cloudy. Add vegetables and herbs, simmer uncovered for approximately 2 hours or until meat is tender. Allow to cool uncovered. Refrigerate overnight. Skim off fat before re-heating.

LIVER CASSEROLE

1 lb. Calves Liver (500 g.)
Water
Salt
1/2 Cup Flour (125 ml.)
6 Tbsp. Vegetable Oil (90 ml.)
3 Medium Onion, sliced
5 Cups Rich Stock (1.1 L.)
1/2 Tsp. Pepper (2 ml.)
1/2 Tsp. Salt (2 ml.)
4 Medium Potatoes, peeled and sliced
2 Medium Apples, peeled and sliced

Cut liver in thin slices. Soak in cold water for 20 minutes. Drain well. Sprinkle liver on each side with salt. Allow to sit for 10 minutes. Rinse in cold water; sponge excess water with paper towels. Coat liver with flour. Reserve remaining flour. Heat oil in a large skillet. Add liver and onions. Cook until browned, turning liver once. Remove liver and onions from pan. Arrange in layers in a baking casserole. Set aside and keep warm. Stir reserved flour into drippings in skillet. Cook for 1 minute, gradually stir in rich stock and bring to a boil. Reduce heat and simmer until sauce has thickened. Season with salt and pepper. Arrange layers of potatoes and apples over liver. Pour sauce over top. Cover tightly. Bake in a 350°F (180°C) oven for 1 1/2 hours or until liver and vegetables are tender.
Serves 6.

PRUNE, POTATO & CARROT TZIMMES

1 Cup Uncooked Prunes (250 ml.)
4 Medium Potatoes
4 Large Carrots (4)
2 Tbsp. Flour (30 ml.)
1/2 Tsp. Salt (2 ml.)
1/4 Cup Shortening (50 ml.)
1/2 Cup Brown Sugar (125 ml.)
1 Cup Water (250 ml.)
1/2 Cup Honey (125 ml.)

Pour boiling water over prunes, cover and leave to sit overnight. Drain. Remove stones from prunes and cut up. Cut potato and carrots in 1/2 inch cubes. Sprinkle with flour and salt. Melt shortening, add carrots and potatoes and cook until shiny tossing occasionally. (about 10 minutes). Add prunes, brown sugar and approximately 3/4 cup of water in which prunes were soaked. Mix thoroughly and place in a 2 quart (20 x 20 cm.) casserole. Bake uncovered in a 350°F (180°C) oven for l hour stirring occasionally. Add honey and bake 20 - 30 minutes longer. *Serves 4 - 6.* *NOTE: If mixture seems too dry, add additional prune water.*

KNISHES

PASTRY:

1 lbs. Shortening (500 g.)
2 Cups Sour Cream (500 ml.)
1 Tsp. Salt (5 ml.)
5 Cups Flour (1.2 L.)

Combine flour and salt in a large bowl. Cut up shortening and work into flour with a pastry blender until crumbly. Add sour cream. Combine well. Form dough into a ball. Divide dough into 6 equal parts. Wrap in plastic wrap and refrigerate for 30 minutes. Roll out one portion of dough at a time into an 8 x 8" (20 x 20 cm.) square. Spread desired filling over dough and roll up like a jelly roll. Cut each roll in 3/4 inch slices. Place on an ungreased baking sheet. Place a small piece of butter or margarine on each Knishe. Bake in a 400°F (200°C) oven for 25 - 30 minutes until golden brown. *Serves 4 - 6 (depending on size).*

POTATO FILLING:

4 Tbsp. Butter (60 ml.)
1 lb. Onions, slices (500 g.)
2 lbs. Potatoes (1 kg.)
1 Tsp. Salt (5 ml.)
1/2 Tsp. Pepper (2 ml.)

Cook potatoes in boiling, salted water until tender. Mash well. Sauté onion in melted butter until transparent. Add to mashed potato and combine well. Season with pepper.

CHEESE FILLING:

2 Cups Dry Cottage Cheese (500 ml.)
1 Egg
1 Tsp. Sugar (5 ml.)
1/2 Tsp. Salt (2 ml.)
1/4 Tsp. Pepper (l ml.)

Beat the cheese with the egg until soft. Season with salt and pepper.

ITALIAN

Collected by MRS. THERESA POLEGATO

RISOTTO (Thick Rice Soup)

6 oz. Chicken Livers (170 g.)
6 oz. Chicken Gizzards (170 g.)
2 Tbsp. Butter (30 ml.)
2 Tbsp. Oil (30 ml.)
2 Tbsp. Tomato Paste (30 ml.)
1 Cup Celery, chopped (250 ml.)
1/2 Tsp. Parsley (2 ml.)
1 Tsp. Allspice (5 ml.)
10 Cups Chicken Stock (2.2L)
2 Cups Rice (500 ml.)
Salt and Pepper to Taste
1/2 Cup Parmesan Cheese, grated (125 ml.)

Heat butter and oil. Add cut up chicken livers and gizzards and fry until browned. Add 2 cups (500 ml.) chicken stock, tomato paste, chopped celery, parsley, allspice, salt and pepper. Simmer 1 hour. Transfer mixture to large pot, place on medium heat. Add rice and remaining chicken stock , one cup (250 ml.) at a time as the rice is cooking. When rice is tender, about 20 - 25 minutes, add grated cheese. Adjust the seasoning and serve. *Serves 8.*

ITALIAN MEATBALLS

1 lb. Ground Beef (500 g.)
1 lb. Ground Pork (500 g.)
1 Egg
1 Onion, chopped
2 Cups Dry Toasted Bread Crumbs (500 ml.)
2 Tsp.Salt (10 ml.)
1 Tsp. Pepper (5 ml.)
1/2 Cup Parmesan Cheese, grated (125 ml.)
2 Tsp. Fresh Parsley (10 ml.)
2 Cloves Garlic, crushed
2 Red Chili Peppers, crushed
4 Tbsp. Milk (60 ml.)
1 Slice White Bread, cubed
2 Tbsp. Oil (30 ml.)
1 Tbsp. Butter (15 ml.

Combine meats, egg, garlic, onion, parsley, salt and pepper in a mixing bowl. Add bread crumbs and cheese. Mix well. Soak one slice of white bread in milk for 10 minutes. Mix to make a paste. Drain off excess milk and add paste to meat mixture. Mix ingredients together. Form meat into desired portions. Makes approximately 30 1 oz. (30 g) meatballs. Heat butter and oil in a large skillet. Brown meatballs, turning frequently. Remove from oil and drain on absorbent paper. Place meatballs in Italian Sauce.

ITALIAN MEATBALL SAUCE

8 Cups Tomatoes, crushed (2 L)
1/2 Cup Tomato Paste (125 ml.)
2 Cups Water (500 ml.)
1 Large Bay Leaf
1 Tsp. Oregano (5 ml.)
1 Tsp. Italian Seasoning (5 ml.)
1/4 Tsp. Parsley (1 ml.)
1/4 Tsp. Basil (1 ml.)
1/4 Tsp. Sugar (1 ml.)
Salt and Pepper to taste

In a large pot, combine crushed tomatoes, tomato paste, water, bay leaf, oregano, italian seasoning, parsley, basil, sugar, salt and pepper. Bring to a boil, reduce heat and simmer for 2 hours. Add the meatballs. Simmer for an additional hour. Serve over spaghetti.

FUASA (Sweet Bread)

3 Tbsp. Yeast (45 ml.)
1 Tsp. Sugar (5 ml.)
3/4 Cup Warm Water (175 ml.)
12 Eggs
2 Cups White Sugar (500 ml.)
2 Cups Milk, scalded (500 ml.)
1 Cup Butter, melted (250 ml.)
1 Tbsp. Artificial Rum Flavouring (15 ml.)
1 Tbsp. Lemon Rind, grated (15 ml.)
2 Large Oranges, grated. Use Rind and Juice
1 Tbsp. Salt (15 ml.)
10 Cups Flour (2.2 L.)

Dissolve sugar and yeast in warm water and allow to sit for 5 minutes. Beat eggs with beater until light. Beat in the sugar until mixture is light and creamy in colour. Add cooled scalded milk, melted butter, yeast mixture, flavouring, lemon rind and juice and rind of oranges and salt. Add enough flour to make a stiff dough. Knead on a floured surface until dough becomes elastic. Put in a large greased bowl and let rise until double in bulk. Divide into four equal pieces and put in greased round pans 8" x 2" (20 cm. x 5 cm.) and allow to rise again. (This will take 1 1/2 to 2 hours) Brush top with melted butter and sprinkle with white sugar. Bake 250°F (120°C) for 1 hour, then 300°F (150°C) for 15 minutes. Turn out on rack to cool.

FRITALE (Deep Fried Cookies)

2 Eggs, beaten
1 Tsp. Vanilla (5 ml.)
2 Small Oranges, rind and juice
3 Cups Sifted Flour (750 ml.)
1 Tsp. Salt (5ml.)
3 Tsp. Baking Powder (15 ml.)
1/2 Cup Chopped Apples or Raisins (125 ml.)

Beat eggs and sugar gradually with vanilla. Add milk, juice and rind of two oranges. Sift flour, salt and baking powder together. Add to egg mixture. Fold in apples or raisins. Mix well. Drop by small spoonfuls into deep hot fat, 375°F (190°C). Fry until crisp. Roll in cinnamon and sugar mixture. *Yields 4 dozen Fritale.*

RIGHT: Dominion Beach

ANTIPASTA

1 Romaine Lettuce, washed and crisped
4 Tomatoes, quartered
10 oz. Tuna Fish, broken in chunks (300 g)
14 oz. Artichoke Hearts, drained (420 g)
8 Slices Ham
8 Slices Salami
8 Radishes
8 Black Olives
1 Tbsp. Parsley, chopped (15 ml.)
1 Tbsp. Capers (15 ml.)

Place romaine leaves on a large platter. Arrange tomatoes, tuna fish, artichoke hearts, salami, ham and radishes on romaine. Arrange radishes, olives, parsley and capers over all. Pour the Italian Dressing over the antipasta and allow to marinate for half hour before serving. *Serves 6.*

ITALIAN DRESSING

1/2 Cup Olive Oil (125 ml.)
3 Anchovy Fillets, mashed
2 Tbsp. Lemon Juice (30 ml.)
Salt and Pepper to Taste.

Combine all ingredients and mix well. Use on antipasta.

PASTA A'LLOUVO (Egg Noodle Dough)

4 Cups Flour (1 L.)
4 Eggs
1 Tsp. Salt (15 ml.)
1/2 Cup Warm Water (125 ml.)

Place the flour and salt on a clean work surface. Make a large indentation in the center of the flour. Break the eggs into the indentation. Add half of the water. Beat the eggs and water with a fork gradually incorporating the flour into the liquid. Add more water if necessary. Work the mixture with your hands until a soft (not sticky) dough is formed. Turn the dough onto a clean work surface and knead for 10 minutes (as you would bread dough). This gives the dough its elasticity. Cover the dough and allow to rest for 30 minutes. Using a rolling pin or pasta machine, divide the dough in two and roll each piece to 1/8 inch thickness. Allow rolled dough to rest for 20 minutes. Cut into desired strips or shapes. Cook pasta in a large pot of boiling, salted water. Fresh pasta cooking time is 3 -4 minutes for 1 lb. (500 g.) of fresh pasta. Drain and serve with desired sauce.

FETTUCINI ALLA ROMANA

1 lb. Fettucini (500 g.)
1 1/2 Cups Light Cream, heated (375 ml.)
6 Tbsp. Soft Butter (90 ml.)
1/2 Cup Grated Parmesan Cheese (125 ml.)
1 Cup Fresh, Frozen Peas, cooked (250 ml.)
1 lb. Prosciutto Ham, cut in thin strips (500 g.)
Pepper, freshly ground

Cook the fettucini in a large pot of boiling, salted water until al dente. Drain fettucini, return to saucepan and add soft butter and parmesan. Toss well together. Add the hot cream, cooked peas, prosciutto and black pepper. Toss well using two forks. Serve immediately. *Serves 4.*
NOTE: The term "al dente" means firm to the bite.

TORALLI (Plain White Cookies)

6 Eggs
1 Cup + 1 Tbsp. Oil (250 ml.) (15 ml.)
1 Cup + 1 Tbsp. Sugar (250 ml.) (15 ml.)
1 Tsp. Vanilla (5 ml.)
5 Cups Flour (1.2 L)

Beat eggs until light. Add oil, sugar and vanilla. Beat until well combined. Add flour, mix well and form into a ball. Roll out dough on a floured surface to 1/4" (1 cm.) thickness. Cut in 1 1/2" (3 cm.) rounds or desired shapes. Place on an ungreased baking sheet. Bake cookies in 350°F (180°C) oven for 10 minutes or until lightly browned.
Remove to cooling rack.
If desired frost with white butter icing and sprinkle with confetti candy.
Note: Toralli freezes well.

ROSETTES (Fry Cakes)
Deep fried cookies, an Italian specialty

12 eggs
1 1/2 Cups Oil (375 ml.)
1 Cup Sugar (250 ml.)
3 Tsp. Baking Powder (15 ml.)
7 1/2 Cups Flour (1.8L)

Beat eggs until light. Beat in oil, sugar. Add baking powder and flour. Form into a ball. Roll out on a floured surface to 3/4" (2 cm) thickness. Cut in strips l" wide (2.5 cm.) by 10 " (25 cm.) long strip and form in a figure 8.
Deep fry in hot oil 375°F (190°C) turning once until browned on both sides. Remove from oil and drain on absorbent paper. Sprinkle with white sugar.
NOTE: It is recommended that these be eaten soon after frying or freeze until needed as they dry out if left out too long.

RIGHT: Wentworth Park, Sydney

GREEK

Collected by MRS. KULA HADJIGEORCHIAU

SALATA (Greek Salad)

1 Head Greens, chopped
Romaine, Endive, Chicory
2 Tomatoes Cut in Wedges
1 Cucumber, sliced
1 Green Pepper , seeded, sliced
2 Green Onions, chopped
2 Small Onion, sliced
6 Radishes, left whole
4 Anchovy Fillets, rinsed
8 Black Olives
1/2 Cup Feta Cheese (125 ml.)
3 Tbsp. Lemon Juice (45 ml.)
1/2 Cup Olive Oil (125 ml.)
1/4 Tsp. Oregano (1ml.)
1/2 Tsp. Salt (2 ml.)
1/2 Tsp. Pepper (2 ml.)
2 Cloves Garlic, crushed
4 Tbsp. Parsley, chopped (60 ml.)
Mint Leaves, chopped

Rub a large wooden salad bowl with garlic. Add prepared vegetables, the anchovies, olives and crumbled feta cheese. Chill. In a small bowl combine lemon juice, olive oil, salt, pepper, oregano, chopped parsley, crushed garlic and chopped mint. mix well. Just before serving, pour dressing over salad and toss.
Serves 6.

SOUVLAKI

2 lbs Boneless Pork or Lamb,
cut in 1 1/2 inch (2-3cm) cubes (1 kg)
Vegetable Oil

MARINADE

1/2 Cup Olive Oil (125 ml.)
1/4 Cup Dry White Wine (50 ml.)
3 Tbsp. Lemon Juice (45 ml.)
1/2 Tsp Pepper (2ml.)
1 Tsp Salt (5 ml.)
1 Tsp. Fresh Oregano, chopped (5 ml.)
1 Tsp. Fresh Mint, chopped (5 ml.)

Place cubed meat in a deep bowl. In a small bowl, combine the marinade ingredients. Pour over meat cubes. Cover and refrigerate for 12 hours, turning meat occasionally while marinating. Prepare a broiler, grill or barbecue. Drain meat, reserving marinade. Slide marinated meat cubes onto 4 long metal or wooded skewers. Place on a grill or under broiler 5 inches from heat (20 cm). Cook for approx. 15-20 min. turning frequently and basting with oil and reserves marinade.
Serve on a bed of rice.

BAKLAVA

1 lb Pkg Frozen Filo Pastry 20 Sheets (500g.)
1 Cup Chopped Walnuts (250 ml)
1 Cup Sliced Almonds Toasted Chopped (250 ml)
1 Cup Butter Melted (250 ml)
1 Tsp Cinnamon (5 ml)
1/2 Tsp Ground Cloves (2 ml)

SYRUP:

2 Cups Sugar (500 ml)
1 Cup Water (250 ml)
1 Cup Honey (250 ml)
Few Drops Lemon Juice

Thaw filo dough and place on clean work table. To prevent filo from drying, cover with a slightly damp cloth or plastic wrap, during preparation time.

FILLING:

Mix the chopped nuts, cinnamon and cloves together.

ASSEMBLY:

Line a 9 X 13 inch (22 X 33cm) pan with half the filo pastry sheets, brushing each sheet with melted butter and pressing well into the corners and the sides. Spread the prepared filling mixture evenly over the pastry and top with the remaining filo pastry sheets, brushing each sheet with melted butter. Press the sheets firmly together at the edges of pan and trim excess with a sharp knife. Brush the top sheet lightly with water , then brush with remaining butter. Score it in about 1/2 inch (2 cm) deep and 2 inches (5 cm) wide diamonds. Bake in a preheated 350°F (180°C) oven for 30 minutes. Reduce heat to 300°F (150°C) and bake for an additional 20 -25 minutes or until top is golden brown.

TO MAKE SYRUP:

In a saucepan, heat the sugar with the water until dissolves. Add honey and lemon juice. Boil for 10 minutes. Cool and chill until very cold.

Upon removing the Baklava from the oven, pour ice cold syrup over it. Carefully insert a knife in the pastry to separate the cuts so syrup will run between the layers. Allow to cool. Serve in diamond shaped pieces.

Note: Filo pastry can be purchased at specialty food shops.

LEBANESE

Collected by MRS. VICTORIA TOMIE
YAKHNIT (Meat & Vegetable Stew)

2 lb. Cubed Lamb or Beef (1 kg)
or 2 lbs Ground Beef (1 kg)
1 Large Onion, chopped
2 Cloves Garlic, chopped
1/2 Tsp. Pickling Spice (2 ml)
3 cups Crushed Tomatoes or Sauce (750 ml.)
3 Cups Frozen or Canned Peas (750 ml)
1 Tsp. Salt (5ml)
1/2 Tsp Pepper (2ml)

Arrange meat in a heavy bottomed deep skillet or saucepan. Brown meat by turning frequently (no oil needed). To meat add onion, garlic, pickling spice, crushed tomatoes or sauce, salt and pepper. bring to a boil, reduce heat and simmer until meat is tender and sauce has thickened - 45 min. Add peas. Simmer for an additional 10 min. Season to taste.   *Serves 6.*

Collected by CAROLYN MORRISON
KAUSA

12 Kusa (Vegetable Marrow) 2 1/2 - 3" (2-3 cm) long
1 1/2 lbs. Lean Ground Beef (750 g)
1/2 Cup Long Grain Rice (125ml)
1 Tsp. Pepper (5 ml)
1 Tsp. Salt (5 ml.)
3 cups crushed tomatoes (750 ml)
2 1/2 Cups Tomato Sauce (625 ml)
2 Cloves Garlic, crushed
1 Tbsp. Garlic Powder (15ml)
1 Tbsp. Cinnamon (15ml)

Cut the end off the vegetable marrow. Remove the center pulp leaving a 1/4" thick wall. In a bowl combine beef, rice, salt, pepper. Mix well and fill the cavity in the center of vegetable marrow with filling. Arrange stuffed marrow in a large baking pan. Combine tomatoes, sauce, garlic and cinnamon. Pour carefully over stuffed marrow. Bake in a 350°F (175°C) oven for 1 hour or until tender.

Collected by MRS. LUCY HANNA
RIZ BISH -SHIRIYYI (Rice & Vermicelli)

3/4 cup vermicelli broken in 1: (5cm. lengths (175ml)
1/4 cup butter (50ml)
1 1/2 cup uncooked long grain rice (375 ml)
3 1/2 cups water (875 ml)
1 Tbsp. salt (15ml)

Melt butter in a heavy saucepan. Add vermicelli and stir continuously until crisp and browned. Rinse rice in cold water, drain and sauté with vermicelli for 1 min. Add water and salt; cover and bring to a boil. Reduce heat and simmer for 20-25 min. stirring occasionally or until rice and vermicelli are tender.   *Serves 6.*

KIBBI

1 1/2 Cups Bulgur (cracked wheat) (375 ml.)
1 Large Onion, grated
2 Tsp. Salt (10 ml.)
1/4 Tsp. Pepper (1 ml.)
Pinch of Cinnamon
Pinch of Allspice
1/2 Cup Butter or Oil (125 ml.)
2 lbs. Ground Lean Lamb or Beef (1 kg.)
1 Tbsp. Melted Butter (15ml.)
1/2 Cup Pine Nuts (125 ml.)

Cover bulgur with cold water. Soak for 1/2 hour. Drain and press between the palm of the hand to remove excess water. Work onion and spices into meat with fingers. Mix well, add bulgur to meat and knead mixture thoroughly. (Dip hands in ice water while kneading in order to soften kibbi. The kneading process is very important. Keep ingredients cold). Grease a 9" x 13" (22 x 33 cm.) pan with oil. Place half of the mixture over bottom of pan, brush with melted butter and sprinkle with pine nuts. Spread remaining meat mixture and flatten well. With a sharp knife score into diamond shaped pieces and run around edge of pan to loosen sides. Make a hole in the center of meat. Pour butter or oil over kibbi. Bake 1/2 hour at 400°F (200°C) oven then reduce heat to 375°F (190°C) and continue to bake for an additional 1/2 hr.
Serves 8. Note: Meat must be ground 3 times to remove all fat.

STUFFED GRAPE LEAVES

1/4 Cup Vegetable Oil (50 ml.)
3 Onions, grated
! Cup Long Grain Rice, uncooked (250 ml.)
1 Cup Pine Nuts (125 ml.)
2 Tbsp Fresh Dill, chopped (30 ml.)
2 Tbsp. Parsley, chopped (30 ml.)
1 Tbsp. Fresh Mint, chopped (15 ml.)
1/2 Tsp. Salt (2 ml.)
1/4 Tsp. Pepper (1 ml.)
1 Tsp. Sugar (5 ml.)
16 Fresh or Preserved Grape Leaves
2 Tbsp. Lemon Juice (30 ml.)
4 Tbsp Butter, melted (60 ml.)
If using fresh grape leaves, bring 1 quart (1 L.) water to a boil.
Dip fresh leaves in boiling water several times to scald.
Immediately rinse under cold running water. Sponge off with paper towel. To use preserved leaves, drain off liquid.

In a large saucpan, heat oil. Add onions & rice. Sauté until onions are transparent. Add hot water, pine nuts, dill, parsley, mint, salt, pepper and sugar. Cover and cook over a low heat for 10-15 min. or until rice is tender. Arrange 4 leaves on bottom of a large baking pan. Arrange remaining leaves on work table with inside up. Place 1 -2 teaspoons (5-10 ml.) of rice mixture on each leaf on work table. Fold leaf sides over the filling; roll up leaves. Arrange rolled stuffed leaves in pan. Sprinkle with lemon juice and brush with butter. Carefully pour 1 cup (250 ml.) of hot water over the leaves. Place a heat proof plate on top of the leaves. Cover and cook in a slow 300°F -325°F (150°C-160°C) oven for 30-40 min. Remove from oven, chill and serve with plain yogurt.

CAPE BRETON CHEFS

Clifford Matthews

A clergyman-teacher turned restaurateur, Clifford operates the 1820 Gowrie House in Sydney Mines, Cape Breton. This historic property has had its share of recognition for its excellence in food service. Among its distinctions are the following: it was rated among the top 100 restaurants in Canada; it was written up in "Where to eat in Canada"; it was the recipient of the T.I.A.N.S. Tourist Association of Nova Scotia Award for 1991. Clifford's original recipes and innovative cuisine have made the Gowrie House a landmark in Cape Breton.

Bernard Lalanne

A native of St-Pierre and Miquelon, Bernard immigrated to Canada in 1951 with his parents who established Nova Scotia's first French restaurant in Halifax called Chez Jean. Bernard worked in the family business. Still following the fine family tradition, he eventually opened his own restaurant in Sydney called Petit Jean. It operated from 1976 until 1989. The Petit Jean restaurant, written up regularly in "Where to Eat in Canada", was a household name and gave visitors as well as local residents an excellent dining experience. Presently manager of Club Forum in Sydney, Bernard still serves his trademark Caesar salad.

On location Goody's Cafe, Cambridge Suites, Sydney

Yvonne LeVert

Cordon Bleu trained, Yvonne has been involved in many different aspects of the food and hospitality industry. Her first career was with the Nova Scotia Department of Agriculture where, as a Home Economist Extension worker, she worked closely with community groups doing food demonstrations. She had her own radio show and did televised food shows. A change of career led to her own televised cooking program called "Cooking with Yvonne". She worked as food director in a large nursing home. The 1987 Canada Winter Games in Cape Breton provided a new challenge: director of food services. Her next project was the opening of La Cuisine des Gourmets, a private cooking school. Cooking and researching cuisines of different countries are to Yvonne a hobby and a profession. She accomplishes this and teaches full time.

Donald MacInnis

Donald grew up in Big Pond, Cape Breton, and is a graduate of the I.W. Akerley Community College culinary program in Dartmouth, Nova Scotia. He did his apprenticeship at the Keltic Lodge in Ingonish, Cape Breton. He has worked extensively in resorts in the Canadian Rockies. A work period in Zurich was a finishing school experience. Donald has been executive chef at the Marklands Inn in Dingwall, Nova Scotia. He also operates a private business in Sydney called Catering Nouvelle.

Gilles Hostal

A native of Lyon, France and a graduate of a French culinary school, Gilles worked in the prestigious Gleneagles Hotel in Scotland. He was also employed by the shah of Iran at his private island estate. Upon immigrating to Canada, he was employed by the Nova Scotia government at the Digby Pines. From there he went to Hotel Newfoundland and was extensively involved in its grand opening. He has been executive chef at the provincially owned Keltic Lodge in Ingonish for the past eight years. The Lodge has received a Four Diamond Rating from the CAA/AAA. It was named a Silver medal Golf Resort in 1989 by *Golf Magazine*. The Keltic dining room, with its panoramic view and excellent cuisine, has pleased guests for many years. Gilles' love of Cape Breton is only surpassed by his love of fine food.

Dundee Resort

63

CLIFFORD MATTHEWS

CHRISTMAS AT GOWRIE HOUSE

TIMBALE OF SOLE WITH MUSSELS

3 lbs. Mussels (1.5 kg.)
1 Cup White Wine (250 ml.)
1 Onion, chopped
2 Tbsp. Butter (30 ml.)
6 - 8 Parsley Sprigs

To prepare mussels, scrub to remove beards. In a large kettle, melt butter, add onion, wine, parsley sprigs and mussels. Shake pot. Cover and cook over high heat until shells open, 3 - 4 minutes. Strain and reserve liquid. Remove mussels from shells and set aside.

CHOU PASTE:

2 Tbsp. Butter (30 ml.)
1/2 Cup Flour (125 ml.)
1/2 Cup Water (125 ml.)
1/2 Tsp. Salt (2 ml.)
2 Eggs

MOUSSE:

1 1/4 Cups Minced Sole (300 ml.)
1/3 Cup Scallops (75 ml.)
3 Eggs
1 1/2 Cups Cream (375 ml.)
1 Tsp. Brandy (5 ml.)
Pinch of Nutmeg
Salt and Pepper to taste

In a small saucepan bring water and butter to a boil. Reduce heat and add flour and salt. Mix well to incorporate flour. Transfer mixture to food processor and add eggs one at a time whisking after each addition. Add scallops and sole and process until smooth. Add salt, pepper, nutmeg and brandy. Slowly, through the spout of processor, add the cream.

VELOUTE SAUCE:

3 Tbsp. Butter (45 ml.)
1/4 Cup Flour (50 ml.)
2 Cups Mussel Liquid (500 ml.)
Pinch of Saffron
1/2 Cup Cream (125 ml.)

Melt butter, add flour. Cook 2 minutes. Whisk in mussel liquid and saffron. Simmer 3 - 5 minutes. Add cream. Adjust seasoning and cool.

ASSEMBLE TIMBALES:

Butter 8 - 6 oz. (175 cm.) moulds. Spread approximately 1/2 cup (125 ml.) mousse on bottom and sides of mould. Spoon in 4 Tsp. (20 ml.) sauce, then 3 or 4 mussels. Add a little more sauce. Spread a covering of mousse over top of mould. Place in a large deep baking pan, pour in simmering water to come up half the sides. Place in a 350°F (180°C) oven 35 minutes. Remove from oven and allow to settle. Unmould onto hot plates. Spoon on remaining hot sauce (re-heated). Garnish with remaining mussels. Enjoy! *Serves 8.*

BROCCOLI BISQUE WITH CURRY

2 Large Bunches of Broccoli
4 Tbsp Butter (60 ml.)
2 Onions, chopped
5 Tbsp. Flour (75 ml.)
1 - 3 Tsp. Curry Powder (5 - 15 ml.)
8 Cups Chicken Stock (2 L.)
Salt, Pepper and Cream

Cut off and discard coarse stems of broccoli. Slice remainder of stems. Separate fleurets. Reserve 1 Cup (250 ml.) for garnish. Steam broccoli for ten minutes. In a 4 quart (4 L.) pot, melt butter, sauté onions. Add flour and cook for several minutes. Add curry and cook 1 minute. Add hot stock. Whisk, cover and simmer 20 minutes. Puree cooked broccoli and add to hot soup. Taste for seasoning. Add a little cream if you wish. Serve garnished with steamed broccoli fleurets. *Makes 10 - 12 servings.*

ROAST TURKEY WITH RICE AND CHESTNUT STUFFING

2 1/4 Cups Brown and Wild Rice Blend (550 ml.)
2 Cups Onion, chopped (500 ml.)
2 Cups Celery, chopped (500 ml.)
1/2 Cup Butter (125 ml.)
1 - 12 oz. Tin Vacuum Packed Chestnuts (375 ml.)
4 Tsp. Fresh Rosemary (20 ml.)
1 Tbsp. Fresh Thyme (15 ml.) or
1 Tsp. each (5 ml.) dried
1 Cup Green Onions, thinly sliced (250 ml.)
1/2 Cup Parsley, chopped (125 ml.)
1 1/2 Cups Fresh Bread Crumbs (375 ml.)
2 Tsp. Salt (10 ml.)
1 - 12 - 14 lbs. Turkey (6 - 8 kg.)
1/2 Cup Butter (250 ml.)

In a large kettle bring 5 cups (1.2 L.) water and salt to a boil. Add rice and boil for 10 minutes. Drain and place in steamer. Steam for 40 minutes. Transfer to a large bowl. In a skillet cook onion and celery with 1/4 cup (50 ml.) of butter. Cook until vegetables are soft. Add to rice. Melt remaining butter, sauté chestnuts, rosemary, thyme, green onion, crumbs and parsley. Cool and combine well with rice mixture.

Rinse turkey and pat dry. Pack the cavity and neck loosely with dressing. Fasten opening with skewers or string. (Bake any excess dressing in a baking dish) Transfer to roasting pan. Baste with 1/4 cup (50 ml.) of melted butter. Cover loosely with foil. Place in a 325°F (160°C) oven allowing 25 - 30 minutes per pound or 50 - 60 minutes per kilogram. Baste every half hour. Remove foil and roast turkey uncovered for the last 45 minutes. Turkey is cooked when internal thermometer reach 180°F (82°C).

Note: If desired, 1 cup (250 ml.) of chicken stock can be added to roaster during baking.

RICH GRAVY

1 Cup Mushrooms, chopped (250 ml.)
1 Cup Chicken or Giblet Stock (250 ml.)
1/4 Cup Fat Drippings from Turkey (50 ml.)
1 Cup White Wine (250 ml.)
1/3 Cup Flour (75 ml.)
3 Cups Chicken Stock (750 ml.)
Salt and Pepper to Taste

In a small saucepan, bring to a boil chopped mushrooms and
1 cup (250 ml.) chicken stock until stock is almost evaporated.
Deglaze the roasting pan with white wine, boil until wine is
reduced by half. In a small saucepan combine drippings and
flour. Cook over medium heat for 2 - 3 minutes. Add
chicken stock, wine mixture and mushrooms. Bring to boil,
reduce heat and cook until gravy thickens and is rich in
colour. Season with salt and pepper.
Note: If giblet stock is used, chop giblet and neck and add to gravy.

PUREE OF WINTER VEGETABLES

8 Medium Potatoes
2 Medium Carrots
3 - 4 Slices Turnip
2 Medium Parsnips
2 Tsp. Salt (10 ml.)
4 Tbsp. Butter (60 ml.)
1/2 Cup Cream, heated (125 ml.)

Prepare vegetables. Place in saucepan. Cover with boiling
water. Add salt. Boil gently until tender. Drain, mash and
add butter, hot cream and whip. *Serves 8.*

BRUSSEL SPROUTS WITH ALMONDS

Clean 2 lbs. (1 Kg.) brussel sprouts. Mark "x" in stem with sharp knife and cook uncovered at gentle boil for 12 - 15 minutes. Drain. Meanwhile in skillet, melt 1/4 (50 ml.) butter. Heat. Add 1/2 cup (125 ml.) almond slices. Continue to sauté until almonds turn golden brown. Transfer sprouts to serving dish. Pour over nuts and butter. Keep hot until service.

BAKED SQUASH

Section one medium to large buttercup squash into serving size sections. Peel and seed. Place in steamer for 12 - 15 minutes. Transfer to baking sheet. Brush with melted butter and maple syrup. Bake for 20 minutes in 350°F (180°C) oven, basting once with butter and syrup before removing from oven.

STEAMED FIG PUDDING WITH RUM BUTTER

1 lb. Smyrna Figs (500 g.)
1 3/4 Cups Milk (425 ml.)
1 1/2 Cups Flour (375 ml.)
2 1/2 Tsp. Baking Powder (12 ml.)
1 Tsp. Nutmeg (15 ml.)
1 Tsp. Cinnamon (15 ml.)
3/4 Tsp. Salt (3 ml.)
3/4 Cup Ground Suet (175 ml.)
1 Cup Butter (250 ml.)
3 Eggs
1 1/2 Cups Fresh Breadcrumbs (375 ml.)
3 Tsp. Grated Orange Rind (15 ml.)

Rinse, stem and chop figs. Combine figs and milk. Bring to a boil and simmer 20 minutes stirring occasionally. Remove from heat and cool. In a bowl combine flour, baking powder, salt, nutmeg and cinnamon. In a bowl, mix together suet and sugar. Add eggs one at a time beating well after each addition. Stir in bread crumbs and orange rind. Add the flour mixture alternately with the cooled fig mixture beating well. Pour into a well buttered 2 quart (2 L.) mould. Cover top with a lid or with foil. Wrap securely with a string, place mould in a large kettle. Add water to halfway up sides of mould. Cover the kettle, bring to boil. Reduce to simmer. Steam the pudding for 2 hours. Remove mould from water and allow to cool 20 minutes. Remove lid or foil. Invert on a serving plate. Serve with Rum Butter.

Note: Fig pudding may be reheated in the microwave.

APRICOT AND ALMOND DACQUOISE

8 Egg Whites
2 Cups Sugar
1 1/2 Cup Nuts (Almond & Brazils) (375 ml.) in food processor with 1/2 Cup (125 ml.) Sugar
Salt and Cream of Tartar

In large metal bowl whip egg whites with 1/2 Tsp. (2 ml.) salt. When frothy add large pinch of cream of tartar. Whip until stiff then slowly add 1 1/2 Cup (375 ml.) sugar a little at a time. On two foil covered baking sheets trace four seven inch (19 cm.) circles. Spread meringue evenly. Place in 250°F (120°C) oven for 1 1/2 hours. Remove from foil. Return to baking sheet and replace in oven with heat turned off for one hour. Remove from oven and set aside.

GANACHE:

8 oz. White Chocolate Chips (250 ml.)
1/3 Cup Whipping Cream (75 ml.)

Melt chocolate chips over hot water. Heat cream to boiling. Remove both from heat. Add hot cream to melted chocolate and whisk together until mixture is thick and creamy.

APRICOT FILLING:

1 1/2 Cups Dried Apricots (375 ml.)
1/3 Cup Sugar (75 ml.)
4 Thin Slices of Orange
1 1/2 - 2 Cups Water (375 ml. - 500 ml.)

In a saucepan, combine apricots, sugar, orange and water. Cook until apricots are tender and water is reduced (mixture will be thick). Process to a thick marmalade consistency.

ASSEMBLY:

Place one circle of meringue on serving plate. Spread with a thin layer of Ganache. Spread some apricot mixture. Repeat this process for remaining circles. Beat 1 Cup (250 ml.) of cream. Add 2 Tsp. (10 ml.) sugar and a few drops of orange flavouring. Spread sides and top of Dacquoise with whipped cream. Sprinkle with toasted almonds. Keep some cream to pipe rosettes on top of Dacquoise.

RUM BUTTER

1 Cup Butter, softened (250 ml.)
1 Cup Demerara Sugar or Brown Sugar (250 ml.)
1/3 Cup Dark Rum (75 ml.)
2 Tbsp. Grated Orange Rind (30 ml.)
Few Grains Nutmeg

In a bowl cream butter and Demerara sugar until light. Slowly add rum, 1 Tbsp. (15 ml.) at a time. Add orange rind and grated nutmeg and continue beating until mixture is fluffy. Transfer to a small bowl.
Makes 2 Cups (500 ml.)

RIGHT: Havenside, Louisbourg

BERNARD LALANNE

ROAST DUCK WITH ORANGE SAUCE

5lb Duck (2.5 kg)

Wash duck, pat dry, sprinkle salt and pepper inside the duck. Place on a rack in roast pan. Place in a 375°F (180°C) oven for 1 1/2 hours, until skin is crisp and brown, and thigh of bird is tender when pierced with a fork. (Drain the fat as it gathers in the pan) Remove duck from oven and keep warm.

ORANGE SAUCE:

1 Cup Sugar (250 ml)
1 Cup Water (250 ml)
1/4 Cup Vinegar (50 ml)
1 Cup Fresh Orange Juice (250 ml)
2 Cups Bordelaise Sauce (500 ml)
Zest of 3 Oranges, cut in strips

To make the caramel, heat sugar in water until dissolved. Bring to a boil and boil steadily to a rich brown caramel colour. Remove from heat. Carefully pour in the vinegar, heat the mixture gently until caramel is dissolved. To the caramel mixture, add orange juice, prepared Bordelaise sauce and zest of oranges (soak orange zest in boiling water before using). Just before serving, baste duck with orange sauce, return to oven for 20 minutes basting every 5 minutes. To serve, cut duck in half or quarters. Ladle sauce over duck and garnish with additional orange slices. *Serves 4-6.*

BORDELAISE SAUCE

2 Tbsp Butter (30 ml)
2 Tbsp Oil (30 ml)
4 Tbsp Flour (60ml)
1 Medium Onion, chopped
2 Medium Carrots, sliced
2 Tbsp Fresh Parsley, chopped (30 ml)
1/4 Tsp Thyme (1 ml)
1 Tsp Salt (5ml)
1/2 Tsp Pepper (2 ml)
1 Tbsp Tomato Paste (15ml)
3 Cups Chicken Stock (750 ml)
1/4 Lemon
3/4 Cup White Wine (175 ml)

Heat butter and oil in a large saucepan, add flour, cook together for 1 minute. Mix in tomato paste. Add onion, carrot, parsley, thyme, salt and pepper. Slowly pour in stock. Combine well. Add lemon. Bring to a boil, reduce heat, simmer for one hour. Strain the sauce. Add wine. Simmer sauce for ten minutes. Taste to adjust seasoning.

CAESAR SALAD

1 Large Head Romaine Lettuce
2 Egg Yolks
2 Cloves Garlic, crushed
1/4 Cup Parmesan Cheese, grated (50 ml)
1/2 Cup Vinaigrette (125 ml)
1 Tsp Worcestershire Sauce (5 ml)
1/2 Cup Sliced Fresh Mushrooms (125 ml)
1/2 Cup Croutons (125 ml)
Black Pepper, freshly ground

Cut base from romaine. Wash greens well in cold water. Wrap in a towel, place in refrigerator to crisp. In a small bowl, combine egg yolks, crushed garlic, parmesan cheese, vinaigrette, Worcestershire sauce. Season with pepper. Rub wooden salad bowl with a piece of garlic. Break crisp greens into bite-size pieces into bowl. Add the dressing, toss to coat greens. Add mushrooms and croutons, and toss again. To serve, garnish with additional parmesan. *Serves 6.*

VINAIGRETTE DRESSING FOR CAESAR SALAD

2 Tbsp Wine Vinegar (30 ml)
6 Tbsp Olive Oil (90 ml.)
2 Tsp Dijon Mustard (10 ml.)
1/4 Tsp salt (1 ml.)
Black Pepper, freshly ground
1/4 Tsp Basil or Thyme (1ml)
Pinch of Sugar

Mix vinegar, mustard, salt, pepper and herbs together. Gradually whisk in the oil until mixture thickens. Add sugar. Use in Caesar salad.

CROUTONS

4 Slices of Bread
4 Tbsp Butter Melted (60 ml.)
1 Clove Garlic

Melt butter and add crushed garlic clove. Simmer for 1 minute. Arrange bread slices on work surface, brush melted butter on bread, turn slice and brush the other side. Cut each slice into cubes. Spread cubes on baking sheet. Place in a 375°F (190°C) oven for 12 - 15 minutes, until croutons are toasted. (Mix croutons on sheet several times during toasting) Serve with Caesar salad.

CREPE SUZETTE

CREPES

1 1/2 Cups Flour (375 ml.)
1/2 Cup Sugar (125 ml.)
1/2 Tsp Salt (2 ml.)
4 Eggs
2 Tbsp Oil (30 ml.)
2 Cups Milk (500 ml.)
Butter as needed.

Measure flour, sugar and salt in a medium-sized bowl. Make a well in the center. Add eggs and beat in the surrounding flour with a spoon, or whisk. When eggs begin to thicken, gradually add half the milk and beat until batter is smooth. Stir in remaining milk, mixing well. Add oil and beat well. Allow batter to rest for 1 hour if time allows. Heat a 6 1/2" (16.5 cm) crepe pan. Brush with melted butter. Carefully ladle 2 tablespoons (30 ml.) of batter in hot pan. Twist the pan clockwise so that the batter quickly coats the whole base of pan. Cook over a medium heat for approximately 1 minute. Turn crepe using a spatula and cook other side. Slide crepe onto a cooling rack and continue the procedure.

FILLING:

1/4 Cup Butter (50 ml.)
1 Cup Icing Sugar (250 ml.)
2 Tbsp Orange Juice (30 ml.)
Grated Rind of 1 Orange
1 oz Cointreau or Grand Marnier (30 g)
Butter and Liqueur as needed.

Cream butter until soft. Add icing sugar, juice and rind of orange. Mix well. Add liqueur. Spread 1 tablespoon (15 ml.) of filling on each crepe. Fold crepe in quarters. Melt 2 tablespoons (30 ml.) of butter in a skillet. Add crepes, roll crepes around in butter, pour some liqueur down side of pan. Ignite with a match. Shake pan until flame has subsided.
Serve 2 crepes per person.
Serves 6.

ABOVE: Wentworth Park, Sydney   RIGHT: Ingonish

YVONNE LEVERT

Instructor, Hospitality
University College of Cape Breton

SPINACH MOULD WITH TOMATO DILL SAUCE

4 Cups Cooked Spinach, well drained (1 L.)
6 Eggs
1 Cup Whipping Cream (250 m.)
2 Tbsp. Butter (30 m.)
1/4 Tsp. Nutmeg (1 ml.)
1 Tsp. Salt (5 ml.)
1 Tsp. Pepper, freshly ground (5 ml.)

Make sure all excess water has been removed from cooked spinach. Chop spinach coarsely. Place in a bowl, add eggs one at a time to the spinach mixing well with a fork. Add the cream, salt, pepper and nutmeg. Mix well. Grease 8 Ramekin dishes with butter and spoon in spinach mixture. Place ramekins in a high sided baking pan. Pour in hot water to halfway up sides. Place in a 300°F (150 °C) oven and cook for 40 - 50 minutes or until firm and tester comes out clean. Serve hot accompanied by Tomato Dill Sauce.
Serves 6.

TOMATO DILL SAUCE

1 Tbsp. Olive Oil (15 ml.)
1 Clove Garlic, crushed
1 Shallot or Small Onion, chopped
1 Tbsp. Tomato Paste (15 ml.)
1 lb. Peeled, Seeded, Chopped Tomatoes (500 g.)
2 Cups Chicken Stock (500 ml.)
1 Tsp. Sugar (5 ml.)
2 Sprigs Fresh Dill
1/2 Tsp. Salt (2 ml.)
Pepper, freshly ground

Heat olive oil in medium sized skillet. Add garlic and chopped onion or shallot. Sauté until onion is soft. Add tomato paste, chopped tomatoes, chicken stock, dill, salt and pepper. Combine well and bring to a boil. Reduce and simmer for 15 - 20 minutes until sauce is reduced and thickened. Puree sauce in food processor. Return to saucepan. Taste to adjust seasoning.

CURRIED PARSNIP SOUP

4 Tbsp. Butter (60 ml.)
1 Med. Onion, finely chopped
1 White of Leek, finely chopped
3 lbs. Parsnips, peeled, diced (1500 g.)
1 Tbsp. Curry Powder (15 ml.)
1 Tsp. Cumin (5 ml.)
6 Cups Chicken Stock (2 L.)
Juice of 1/2 Lemon
1 Tsp. Salt (5 ml.)
Black Pepper, freshly ground as needed
1 Cup Light Cream (250 ml.)
2 Tbsp. Natural Yogurt (30 ml.)
2 Tbsp. Fresh Parsley, chopped (30 ml.)

Melt butter in large pot and sauté onion, leek and parsnip for 5 minutes. Add curry powder and cumin and cook for an additional 2 minutes, stirring continuously to prevent vegetables from sticking. Add chicken stock and lemon juice. Bring to a boil, reduce heat and simmer the soup for approximately 30 minutes until parsnip is tender. Remove from heat and puree in food processor. Return to pot. Season and re-heat. Add the heated cream just before serving, do not boil. To serve, garnish with a swirl of yogurt and chopped parsley.
Serves 6.

RHUBARB/CRANBERRY SORBET

1 cup Cranberries (250 ml.)
1 Cup diced Rhubarb (250 ml.)
1/2 Cup White Wine (125 ml.)
1/2 Cup Water (125 ml.)
3/4 Cup Sugar (150 ml.)
4 Tbsp. Lemon Juice (60 ml.)

Trim rhubarb stalks and cut stalks in small pieces. In a saucepan combine rhubarb, cranberries, sugar water and lemon juice. Bring to a boil and cook for 10 - 15 minutes until rhubarb and cranberry mixture is soft. Puree in food processor for 1 minute. Pour mixture in a shallow container (not aluminum) and place in freezer. When mixture is partially frozen, break up and stir gently with a fork. Repeat this procedure several times until mixture becomes grainy. Spoon sorbet into a container. Cover lightly and freeze until needed. Serve a small amount in crystal dishes. Garnish with fresh mint leaves.
Serves 6.

POACHED SALMON WITH LEEK AND RED PEPPERCORN SAUCE

6 Medium Salmon Steaks (6 oz. each)
1 Cup White Wine (250 ml.)
2 Cups Cold Water (500 ml.)
1 Large Onion, sliced
6 Peppercorns
1 Bay Leaf
1 Sprig Dill

LEEK AND PEPPERCORN SAUCE

10 Red Peppercorns
1 Large Leek, sliced
3 Tbsp. Butter (45ml.)
1 Small Garlic Clove, crushed
3 Tbsp. Flour (45ml.)
1 Cup Fish Stock (250 ml.)
1/2 Cup White Wine (125 ml.)
1/2 Cup Cream, heated (125 ml.)
Salt and Pepper as needed

Arrange salmon steaks in a single layer in a large skillet or roast pan. Pour wine and water over steaks. Add onion, peppercorns, bay leaf and dill. Bring to a boil. Reduce and simmer uncovered for 10 - 15 minutes or until steaks are cooked. Remove steaks from stock. Place on a warm plate to keep warm. To prepare sauce, melt butter in medium skillet. Add sliced leeks, peppercorns and garlic. Cook over medium heat stirring occasionally until leeks are soft, 5 - 8 minutes. Add flour and cook over medium heat stirring for 1 minute. Remove from heat. Gradually stir in the stock and white wine. Stir constantly until sauce boils and thickens. Reduce heat, gradually add the heated cream while stirring. Season with salt and pepper.
Serves 6.

SHORTBREAD WITH LEMON CURD, CANDIED PEEL AND WILD BLACKBERRY COULIS

RICH LEMON CURD:

6 Eggs
1 1/2 Cups Sugar (375 ml.)
2 Tbsp. Grated Lemon Rind (30 ml.)
2/3 Cup Lemon Juice (150 ml.)
1/2 Cup Butter (125 ml.)

Combine eggs, sugar, rind and juice in a bowl. Place over a pan of hot water on medium heat. Stir until mixture is thick. Transfer to cold bowl and whisk in the butter a little at a time. Cool, cover and refrigerate.

SHORTBREAD:

2 1/2 Cups Flour (625 ml.)
1 Cup Sifted Icing Sugar (250 ml.)
1 Cup Butter (250 ml.)
2 Egg Yolks (2)
2 Tsp. Lemon Rind (10 ml.)
1 Tbsp. Water (15ml.)
1/2 Tsp. Vanilla (2 ml.)

Combine flour in a bowl. Rub butter gently into flour with fingertips until mixture is like crumbs. Mix egg yolks, rind, water and vanilla. Add to flour mixture and mix to combine. Form mixture into ball. Wrap and refrigerate for 30 minutes. Roll out the dough to 1/4 inch (2.5 mm.) thickness. Cut 3 inch (8 cm.) circles and place on lightly greased baking tray. Bake in a 300°F (150°C) oven for 20 - 30 minutes or until lightly browned. Cool on tray for 5 minutes before transferring to rack to cool.

CANDIED PEEL:

5 Lemons
2 Grapefruit
1 1/2 Cups Sugar (375 ml.)
1 1/2 Cups Water (375 ml.)

Peel rind thinly from lemons and grapefruit using a vegetable peeler. Remove any pith (white substance from peel). Cut rind into thin strips. Place rind in saucepan. Cover with water. Bring to a boil, drain and repeat twice. Place sugar and water in pan. Stir over heat without boiling until sugar is dissolved. Simmer 1 minute. Add rind and simmer over heat for approximately 10 minutes or until rind is clear. Cool. Use rind as a garnish with dessert. (Rind can be prepared two days ahead of time and kept in a sealed container in refrigerator)

BLACKBERRY COULIS:

2 Cups Blackberries (500 ml.)
1 Cup Cold Water (250 ml.)
3/4 Cup Sugar (150 ml.)
1 Tsp. Lemon Rind (5ml.)

Combine blackberries, water, sugar and lemon rind in a small saucepan. Bring to a boil and simmer until berries are soft. Cool slightly. Process in food processor for 1 minute. Strain and chill.

TO ASSEMBLE:

Ladle Blackberry Coulis on half of the plate. Place one shortbread on each serving plate. Top with a large spoonful of lemon curd and a small amount of candied peel. Place a shortbread on top. Dust with icing sugar. Decorate with more candied peel, candied syrup and fresh mint.

POTATO FLORETS

6 Large Potatoes
2 Tbsp. Butter (30 ml.)
1/2 Cup Cream Cheese (125 ml.)
2 Tbsp. Milk (30 ml.)
1 Tsp. Salt (5 ml.)

Peel potatoes. Cut in quarters. Cook in water until tender.
Combine butter, cream cheese and milk in a small saucepan.
Place over low heat to melt cheese and butter. Drain
potatoes and whip in electric mixer. Add cheese mixture and
beat until light and creamy. Season with salt and pepper. Fill
a large pastry bag with star tube attachment with potato
mixture. Pipe out small rosettes of potatoes on a lightly
buttered baking sheet. Set oven to 375°F (190°C) and bake
until rosettes are golden (12 - 15 minutes).
Serve 3 - 4 per serving.
Serves 6.

MEDLEY OF GLAZED VEGETABLES

4 Medium Carrots
1 Small Turnip
1 Small Cucumber
4 Tbsp. Butter (60 ml.)
8 Sugar Cubes
2 Tbsp. Hot Water (30 ml.)
Salt and Pepper to taste

Peel carrots and turnip and cut in long strips. Cut the
cucumber in long strips (do not peel). Bring a saucepan of
water to a boil. Add carrots and turnip. Boil for 1 minute,
drain and plunge vegetables in cold water and drain. Melt
butter in a skillet over medium heat. Add sugar cubes. Stir
cubes with a fork to dissolve. Add hot water, stir well. Add
carrots, turnip and cucumber and carefully turn vegetables
around in the syrupy mixture to glaze. This will take 4 - 5
minutes. Season with salt and pepper. *Serves 6.*

Barrachois River

DONALD MACINNIS

SALT CODFISH DAUPHINE

1/2 lb. Salt Cod, cooked (250 gm.)
4 Cups Dry Mashed Potatoes (1 kg.)
2 oz. Chopped Fresh Chives (55 gm.)
1 Diced Shallot

Finely flake the cod and mix all ingredients together.

CHOU PASTE

1 Cup All Purpose Flour (250 ml.)
1 Cup Milk or Water (250 ml.)
1/3 Cup Butter (75 ml.)
Pinch of Salt
4-5 Eggs

In a heavy saucepan bring to a boil milk or water and butter.
Lower heat. Add salt and flour all at once. Stir quickly until
smooth. Stir the mixture until dry. (It should fall away from
the sides of the saucepan). Remove from heat. Let stand for
2 - 3 minutes. When mixture is slightly cooled, add eggs, one
at a time, beating vigorously after each addition (batter will
be thick and shiny).

TO COMPLETE THE SALT CODFISH DAUPHINE:

Fold in 2 parts fish recipe to 1 part choux paste recipe. Shape
mixture as desired. Preheat deep fryer to 350 °F (180°C)
Deep fry until golden brown.
Serves 6.

GREENS WITH MAPLE GARLIC DRESSING

1 oz. Cape Breton Maple Syrup (30 ml.)
1 Egg yolk
1 Shallot, diced
1 Clove Garlic, diced
1 Sprig Fresh Chive, diced
2/3 Cup Canola Oil (150 ml.)
1/4 Cup Red Wine Vinegar (50 ml.)
Salt and Freshly Ground Pepper, to taste
1 Head Romaine Lettuce, washed

Place egg yolk in a stainless steel bowl and add diced shallot.
Slowly whisk in oil to emulsify, i.e., as for mayonnaise. Add
the vinegar and remaining ingredients. Let stand overnight.
Break romaine in a bowl; toss with dressing.
Serves 6.

WHITE BEAN AND POTATO SOUP

1 lb. Pork Tenderloin (500 g.)
1/2 lb. White Dried Beans (250 g.)
1 Med. Potato
1 Med. Onion
1 Clove Garlic
2 oz. Red Wine (55 g.)
1 Sprig Fresh Thyme
Salt and Freshly Ground Pepper, as needed
Paprika, as needed

Cut pork in 1/2 inch cubes. Season with salt and freshly
ground pepper. Lightly flour the pork and brown in a
medium sized skillet. Add onion, garlic and paprika.
Sauté slightly and add red wine. Reduce red wine by half.
Remove ingredients from skillet and place in a medium sized
casserole Slightly cover with water and chicken stock. Season
broth and add white beans and potato. Bake 3 hours in 300 °F
(150°C). oven. To serve add molasses dumplings and 2 - 3
Tbsp./15 ml. of syrup.
Serves 6.

MOLASSES DUMPLINGS

1 Cup Flour (250 ml..)
1 1/2 Tsp. Baking Powder (6 ml..)
Pinch Salt
Cold Water to Moisten

Combine ingredients and add just enough cold water to
make a sticky consistency.

SYRUP:

1 Cup Molasses (250 ml.)
3 Tbsp. Butter (45 ml.)
1 1/2 Cups Water (375 ml.)
2 Tbsp. Vinegar (30 ml.)

Combine molasses, butter, water and vinegar. Bring to a
rolling boil. Add heaping spoonfuls of dumpling batter.
Cook until dumplings are double in size and dry.
Serve with Bean and Potato Soup.

RIGHT: On location at the Markland Resort, Dingwall

LAMB WELLINGTON IN ROSEMARY BANNOCK

4 - 6 oz. Portions Fresh Cape Breton Loin of Lamb (640 g.)
2 oz. Fresh Mushrooms, diced (55 g.)
1 Medium Shallot, diced
1 oz. Dry Red Wine (30 ml.)
Salt and Freshly Ground Pepper

Lightly season the lamb and brush with oil. In a med. to high heated skillet, sear the lamb. Remove lamb from skillet, set aside to cool. Discard fat from pan and add red wine to pan and simmer. Add chopped mushrooms and shallot. Cook until liquid is reduced to 1/4 (almost dry). Set aside to cool.

ROSEMARY BANNOCK

1 Tbsp. Fresh Rosemary, chopped (15 ml.)
2 Cups Flour (500 ml.)
1 1/4 Tsp. Baking Powder (6 ml.)
1/2 Tsp. Baking Soda (2 ml.)
Pinch of Salt
6 Tbsp. Butter (90 ml.)
3/4 Cup Sour Milk (175 ml.)

Sift together all the dry ingredients. Cut in the butter with a fork until it becomes flaky. Quickly whisk in sour milk. Place dough on lightly floured surface and knead 2 - 3 minutes. Roll out dough to 1/2 inch thickness. Cut the dough into 4 pieces (big enough to wrap l portion of lamb). Place lamb in center of dough. Spoon on chilled mushroom mixture. Wrap the lamb and brush with melted butter. Bake 350 °F (180°C) until golden brown.

CORDELLA'S CHOCOLATE AND WILD MINT TORTE

1/2 Cup Butter, softened (125 ml.)
3/4 Cup Sugar (175 ml.)
1 Tsp. Vanilla (5 ml.)
7 Eggs, Separated
1/3 Cup Flour (75 ml.)
3 Tbsp. Cornstarch (45 ml.)
2 oz. Chocolate (60 g.)
1 Tbsp. Vegetable Oil (15 ml.)
1 Tbsp. Wild Mint, finely chopped (15 ml.)

Cream the butter and 1/4 Cup sugar (50 ml.) along with vanilla. Slowly add the egg yolks. Combine flour and cornstarch and mix into batter. Divide the batter in two separate bowls. Melt chocolate and oil in double boiler and add to one bowl of batter. Add chopped mint to other bowl of batter. Whisk egg whites until stiff. Add remaining sugar and continue beating until they form a peak. Divide egg whites between each batter. Grease a 9 inch (22 x 5 cm.) round pan or line with parchment paper. Using a large spoon, layer the pan with approximately 1 oz. of chocolate mixture. Place under broiler for 2 - 3 minutes until cooked. Repeat this process with the mint batter, spooning over cooked chocolate batter (you need not wait for batter to cool before spooning next batter). Repeat process alternating layers until batter is used up. Allow torte to cool and sprinkle with icing sugar.
Serves 6 - 8.

ABOVE: Glenora Falls   RIGHT: Dingwall

GILLES G. HOSTAL

EXECUTIVE CHEF
KELTIC LODGE, Ingonish

CHILLED LITTLE TURNED SUMMER VEGETABLE PLATTER

2 Small Zucchini, cut 1" long pieces
1 Med. Turnip, cut 1" long pieces
2 lg. Carrots, cut 1" long pieces
1 Large Head Broccoli, cut in florets
1 Small Cauliflower, cut in florets
16 Mushrooms, cut in quarters
8 Cherry Tomatoes
1 Large Onion, chopped
1 Tbsp. Whole Coriander (15 ml.)
1 Tbsp. Butter (15 ml.)
1 Tbsp. Curry Powder (15 ml.)
2 Cups White Wine (500 ml.)
2 Cups Lemon Juice (500 ml.)
2 Cups Olive Oil (500 ml.)
1 Stock Celery
2 Bay Leaves
Tied together in
1 Bunch Thyme, in a bundle

Sauté onion in butter with curry powder and coriander. Cook for 1 minute. Add white wine, lemon juice, olive oil, bundle of herbs and cook for 10 minutes. Season to taste. Cook each vegetable individually in the broth until tender but firm. Blanch broccoli in salted water (broccoli would loose its color if cooked in broth). Marinate broccoli in broth for 1 hour before serving. Cool vegetables and broth and arrange vegetables on a plate. Pour broth over vegetables.
Serves 8.

ALMOND CREAM SOUP WITH AMARETTO LIQUEUR

1/2 Cup Whole Almonds, shelled and peeled (125 ml.)
8 Cups Chicken Stock (2 L.)
1/4 Cup Rice (125 ml.)
1 Medium Leek (1)
1/4 Cup Whipping Cream (50 ml.)
4 Egg Yolks
1 Tbsp. Amaretto (15 ml.)
1/4 Cup Toasted Sliced Almonds (50 ml.)

Cook almonds, rice and chopped leek with chicken stock for about 45 minutes (once mixture boils, turn heat to simmer). Puree mixture in a blender until smooth. Mix cream and egg yolks. Bring soup to a near boil. Add cream and egg yolk mixture to soup, stirring constantly. Cook for 1 minute - Do Not Boil. Season to taste and add liquor. Return to blender to obtain a smooth creamy texture.
Serve in soup plates topped with toasted almonds.
Serves 8.

RASPBERRY SCHOONER GRANITE

1 Cup Raspberry Puree (250 ml.)
1 1/2 Cup Schooner Beer (375 ml.)
3 Cups Sugar (750 ml.)
2 Cups Water (500 ml.)

Boil together water, raspberry puree and sugar until sugar is dissolved. Remove from heat. Add the beer and combine well. Pour the granite mixture in a flat plastic container and place in the freezer. When it starts to freeze, scrape the granite with a fork repeating this technique several times until granite is granular in texture. Arrange in dishes and garnish with mint leaves and fresh raspberries.
Serves 8.

CHARBROILED NEIL'S HARBOUR SWORDFISH FILLETS

With a Rainbow of Red, Yellow and Green Pepper Sauce

8 - 6 oz. Swordfish Steaks (170 gm.)
1 1/2 Cups White Wine (375 ml.)
1 1/2 Cups Cream (375 ml.)
1 lb. Unsalted Butter (500 g.)
1 Tbsp. Shallots, chopped (15 ml.)
Juice of 1/2 Lemon
1 Yellow Pepper
2 Green Pepper
1 Red Pepper
1 oz. Spinach (30 g.)

Boil yellow, red and green peppers in salted water for approximately 20 minutes. Cool and peel off the skin. Puree each individually in blender and set aside. Blanch spinach. Process in blender and combine with green pepper to obtain a nice color.
Serves 8.

TO PREPARE BUTTER SAUCE:

Put chopped shallots, lemon juice and white wine in a skillet and reduce to 1/4 amount. Add cream and reduce for a few minutes. Cut butter in cubes. Add slowly to the mixture over medium heat continuously whisking until a smooth sauce is obtained. Divide butter sauce in saucepans. Add different coloured pepper puree to each saucepan. Keep warm. Season swordfish. Charbroil until cooked. To serve, arrange sauces on plate like a rainbow. Place fish and garnish with vegetable flowers.
Serve immediately.
Serves 8.

THE FALL WATER LILY

CHOCOLATE WAFER CUP:

1/2 Cup Butter (125 ml.)
1/2 Cup Icing Sugar (125 ml.)
1/2 Cup Flour (125 ml.)
3 Egg Whites
1/4 Tsp. Vanilla Extract (1 ml.)
2 Tbsp. Cocoa (30 ml.)

In a small bowl combine flour, icing sugar and cocoa powder. Add egg whites one at a time mixing after each addition. Add the vanilla and the partially cooled melted butter. Mix well. Cool batter in fridge for 30 minutes. Design on a piece of cardboard a waterlily flower. Grease a baking sheet. Use waterlily design like a stencil on baking sheet. Spread batter with spatula on stencil. Bake in a 400°F (200°C) oven for 7 minutes. Remove quickly and place of an overturned bowl to shape. Repeat process until batter is used up. Set wafers aside to cool.

APPLE MOUSSELINE

1 Cup Apple Juice (250 ml.)
1/2 Cup Apple Cider (125 ml.)
3 Egg Yolks
4 Tbsp. Custard Powder or Cornstarch (50 ml.)
1/2 Vanilla Bean
5 Tbsp. Sugar (75 ml.)
1 Cup Whipping Cream (250 ml.)
3 Gelatin Leaves

Boil together apple cider, apple juice and vanilla bean. Mix together egg yolks, sugar, custard powder or cornstarch. Pour boiled apple juice over egg mixture. Return to burner and cook over a medium heat until mixture thickens. Remove from heat. Soak gelatin leaves until soft in cold water. Squeeze out excess water and add to pastry cream. Refrigerate until well chilled. Whip cream and fold into pastry cream. Refrigerate for l hour before serving.

GOLDEN JELLY

1 3/4 Cup Apple Juice (425 ml.)
4 Tbsp. Apple Cider (60 ml.)
Juice of l Lemon
3/4 Cup Sugar (175 ml.)
8 Gelatin Leaves

Soak gelatin leaves until soft in cold water. Heat apple juice and apple cider and juice of lemon until warm. Add gelatin leaves and stir. Pour 4 Tbsp. (60 ml.) on each dessert plate and place in refrigerator until firm. Place the chocolate wafer tulip on centre of plate. Using a piping bag, fill the tulip with Apple Mousseline. Decorate with chocolate curls, mint leaves and orange zest. *Note: 6 leaves of gelatin equals 1 Tbsp. (15 ml.) of granulated gelatin.*

ABOVE: Mary Ann Falls, Ingonish   RIGHT: Keltic Lodge, Ingonish

NEL FIELD

WARREN GORDON

Master of Photographic Arts

Since 1973, Warren Gordon has operated Gordon Photographic Limited a major photographic studio and scenic gallery in downtown Sydney. His studio handles a wide spectrum of photographic assignments ranging from portraits and family groups to industrial and aerial photography. He has received regional and national recognition for his work, including the degree of Master of Photographic Arts.

In 1986, Mr. Gordon became associated with Comstock, a large stock photo agency based in Toronto and New York. In pursuit of new and unique images for this agency, expeditions throughout Canada, Asia, Europe, the Caribbean and the Rocky Mountains have been undertaken.

He has published six books of his Cape Breton photographs — *Images of Cape Breton* in 1981 and *Cape Breton Island of Islands* in 1985 — both of which have received an enthusiastic response, as well as *Cape Breton Address Book* in 1988 and *Cape Breton, A Place Apart* in 1989. *Jewel of the Atlantic…The Nova Scotia Story* was published in 1990 and *Cape Breton Portfolio* was released in December 1991. Mr. Gordon's book "*Island of Ghosts*" was produced in 1992.

YVONNE LEVERT

Cordon Bleu Chef

Having pursued a successful career as a teacher, Chef de Cuisine Yvonne Le Vert has combined a lifelong love of cooking and food research in her efforts to capture the true essence of Cape Breton cuisine and its people. A native of Margaree Forks and of Acadian parents, she is a graduate Home Economist who later attended the prestigious Académie du Cordon Bleu de Paris in the French capital where she obtained the Grand Diplôme. She is a member of the Cape Breton Chapter, Canadian Association of Chefs de Cuisine, and also a member of La Confrérie de la Chaîne des Rôtisseurs. She is presently employed as an instructor in the Hospitality Administration program at the University College of Cape Breton.

SPECIAL THANKS TO:
Judy Abraham: Typing and Proofreading,
Bernard LeVert: Taster and Sampler,
and Paul Comeau, John Lalanne, Nel Field and
Marjorie MacQueen for their advice and support.

INDEX